Simple Tools

Simple Tools

**Digital resources
in your classroom**

MARTIN JORGENSEN

Copyright © Martin Jorgensen 2022

All rights reserved. No part of this book may be reproduced or transmitted in any form or by any means, electronic or mechanical, including photocopying, recording or by any information storage and retrieval system, without prior permission in writing from the publisher.

Published by Amba Press
Melbourne, Australia
www.ambapress.com.au

Editor – Rica Dearman
Cover designer – Alissa Dinallo

Printed by IngramSpark

ISBN: 9781922607201 (pbk)
ISBN: 9781922607218 (ebk)

A catalogue record for this book is available from the National Library of Australia.

Contents

Introduction		1
Chapter 1	**Starting with what you know**	7
	Learning routines	8
	Why digital tools are useful	10
Chapter 2	**Establishing a foundation**	17
	Digital resources with a clear purpose	19
	Thinking routines	21
	Other common thinking routines	24
	Interaction phases	26
Chapter 3	**Finding simple tools**	29
	Time and big platforms	30
	Tool choice	35
	Digital tool design	37

Chapter 4	**Judging the load**		45
	The limits of working memory		46
Chapter 5	**Create and discover**		55
	Creative discovery		57
Chapter 6	**Routines and features**		65
	Discussion tools		65
	Mapping tools		68
	Sequencing tools		69
	Connection tools		71
	Reflection tools		73
Chapter 7	**Transitions**		75
	Transition in a learning sequence		76
	Reflection for students		79
	Reflection is for teachers, too!		84
	An elephant in the room		88
Chapter 8	**Collaboration and discussion online**		93
Conclusion			109
Acknowledgements			113
References			115

Introduction

Many years ago, when I started my career in education, I was struck very quickly by just how hard it was to find the right digital tools for my classroom. As my experience grew and I had the fortunate opportunity to work with some particularly gifted educators and observe their practice, I began to appreciate that in the same way that some of the principal theories in education have been adapted from other disciplines, many of the digital tools we were using with our students were also designed for other contexts first and then adapted to F-12 educational markets as an afterthought.

Many of the digital tools we used simply weren't designed for young people or classrooms, and I had witnessed some fairly spectacular failures in the use of digital tools that simply were not fit for purpose.

I didn't have a clear method that I could employ as I chose the right digital tools for my classroom. I had a common-sense approach, however, like most teachers, which often worked in my favour. Failure didn't stop me trying, but I came across many teachers for whom the digital tools had become peripheral at best because of repeated frustrations. Often, they had been burnt so many times and wasted so much classroom time trying to get them to work that their consensus was that it simply wasn't worth the trouble.

There is a great deal else to contend with in a classroom without having to navigate problematic software as well. I increasingly found myself leaning towards simpler tools – digital tools that did only one thing, but did it well.

I found that by choosing simple tools, their connection to my own pedagogical approach and to how I best employed them with specific content was more clearly understood by me and by my students. It was also precisely because of their simplicity in design and clear purpose that I was able to employ those same tools in increasingly complex ways.

As my career shifted towards a growing interest in the place of digital tools in classrooms, I began working with teachers and schools to support them in reflecting on the implications of the choices they were making in the selection of digital tools. There, too, I was lucky enough to observe the challenge faced by teachers just like me, and to work with schools faced with choices over which platforms they should become wedded to, and which digital tools to lean towards.

Some chose single-system solutions like Google, but more often I witnessed schools adopt a myriad of programs that were threaded together in an often complex and sometimes haphazard learning ecosystem. Many schools in my experience would lurch from one digital resource to the next over the years, with each new digital tool often championed by a handful of teachers, but rarely universally adopted.

The difficulty in finding digital resources that suit a myriad of pedagogical styles and a range of content complexities is something schools worldwide struggle with. Some simply opt for a single answer, making themselves a 'Google school' or something similar, locking down their choices to only what is offered within a single suite of options. Others commit to a platform like Moodle or Canvas, or work with a patchwork of digital classroom solutions.

As my career progressed and I moved into a role leading digital learning in the largest F-12 school in the state, Virtual School Victoria, I quickly discovered that virtual schooling offered many of the same difficult choices as bricks-and-mortar schools. Virtual environments were often complex considerations for students and teachers. As the years rolled on, my appreciation for the use of simple digital tools deepened, and my awareness of their impact on both pedagogy and student outcomes continued to develop.

When the pandemic struck in 2020, I was working as an assistant principal and saw teachers across the world suddenly placed in an abrupt position where they had to use a range of digital tools in ways that provided new challenge. Schools were forced to select resources to support remote delivery quickly, and the choices they may have made over far longer periods were rushed forward to support a change in practice. For many teachers, their classroom practice was frequently not quickly or easily adaptable to their new digital toolkit, nor did they often have an appropriate theoretical model to reach for in transitioning their practice.

Many teachers from my perspective often lacked a consistent approach that allowed them to employ the best of their existing pedagogy and content knowledge with digital tools that were clearly recognisable as fit for purpose.

There remains a notable lack of evidence in virtual learning about what might be considered effective practice. The research base for online learning is maturing and still relatively young, but there are a few things that we can observe from the research thus far.

There is clearly a need to adapt traditional classroom practice, and the job of the teacher in virtual settings in particular includes new roles that are akin to instructional designers and 'interaction facilitators'.

This book represents my personal view and is an attempt to draw together an approach to bridge this gap – one developed from my work with schools across the state, my work with teachers with exceptional practice and drawing on well over a decade of work in exclusively online classrooms in a large, virtual F-12 school.

It is an approach that I feel empowers teachers and students in the use of digital tools. It encourages metacognitive reflection and is better suited to the critical considerations of cognitive load and its significant impact on student learning. Digital tool literacy is a foundational skill to be pursued like any other in the curriculum.

This is not a book in which to list resources for the classroom, it's a framework for thinking about how you use your technology and how to select digital tools for purposeful pedagogical application.

At its heart, this book is about a few key ideas:

1. Selecting digital tools that have a clear purpose and do one thing well allows us to discern their appropriate alignment more easily with content and a pedagogical approach.
2. Simple tools of this nature can aid in reducing cognitive load, demanding less of working memory.
3. Classroom routines and visible thinking routines can be a logical place to consider introducing more complex uses for simple digital tools, accommodated by their often-nimble nature and clear purpose.
4. By employing this type of digital tool, teacher and student time in the classroom is economised and a greater clarity of purpose in the use of those tools is possible for both teacher and student.

This book is less of a blueprint and more of a jumping-off point. It is a series of recommendations and advice illustrating how to best understand and pursue the points above.

Each chapter offers an opportunity to observe an issue, a range of solutions and ways of understanding that issue, and is often accompanied by explicit examples. I've then broken the chapters down into key 'takeaways' accompanied by an executive summary. Often chapters will be coupled with an activity that you can use to practice some of the ideas that rest within the ideas we've explored.

For example:

Outline of an issue
↓
Broad solution
↓
An explicit example
↓
Key chapter takeaways
↓
Sum it up (executive summary)
↓
Put it into action (goal setting)

In each chapter, I'll also encourage you to take an action that puts into practice what you've learnt. I encourage you to consider two principles as you work through each section: forgive and return.

Forgive – because it can be hard to stay the course when you're working through change. Life happens to all of us, it throws us off-kilter and other priorities compete for and often win our attention in spite of our best efforts. When you feel you've not stayed the course and let the goal or change you wanted to see slip away, forgive yourself. We're only human!

Return to the goal you'd set and move forwards. Changing practice is hard, and real change takes time and is won in a thousand small battles rather than one big concerted effort. Raking over the regret of not having accomplished what you wanted takes a good deal of time and energy. I'd respectfully suggest that you skip the self-recrimination and simply return to the task at hand. Often, nobody is watching, except you. Remind yourself why you're working towards the goals you've set yourself and return to the key consideration that sits at the centre of the work: your students.

Learning is a complex undertaking. As Richard Elmore from the Harvard Graduate School of Education puts it: "Teaching is not rocket science. It is, in fact, far more complex and demanding work than rocket science." (*The Age*, 2007)

If you are relatively new to the use of digital tools in your classroom, I hope that you find *Simple Tools* an accessible and useful approach to digital tool use as you wrestle with the complex choices ahead.

If you are more experienced in the use of digital tools in your classroom, then you already know the benefit of drawing upon the best of what is around you, and I hope that you'll take what you need from this book.

Either way, I'd love to hear your feedback and stories of how you have approached digital tool use in the classroom. Teaching with technology is complex, and I hope that you'll find *Simple Tools* provides a more straightforward path through some of that complexity.

CHAPTER 1

Starting with what you know

Consider for a moment the routines in your classroom that you employ every day. Some of them are established thinking routines, while others will be purposeful pedagogical approaches formed from your own research – and may include habits formed over the course of your teaching career.

You might also be thinking about simple rituals, such as the way you greet the students as they enter your classroom – you might start the day welcoming them by name, establishing rapport and reinforcing they are in a safe space in which to learn. And you might also be thinking about more complex thinking routines you employ as your class gets under way, routines you use to guide your students as they develop new knowledge and new understandings to build skills and encounter new ways of thinking.

These routines, both simple and complex, are the foundation of your classroom and provide a framework for learning. They are also often employed to reinforce to your students that structured ways of thinking have value.

It seems only right then, that the technology you use should complement these structures. You know what you want to teach, and you know how you intend to pursue it. You need technology you can call on that offers flexibility and that fits with your routines and planning; technology you can reinvent and repurpose quickly when the need arises, where you see an opportunity or where an unanticipated student need or learning opportunity emerges. You also need a way of finding and applying these adaptable and flexible tools, and you need a method of employing them effectively that recognises and draws on your existing practice.

How then to begin, to choose which digital tools to use?

There are large platforms that offer a range of promises, all conveniently packaged within a learning ecosystem that offers a single solution to all your needs. Platforms such as Blackboard, Moodle, Google Classroom and Canvas, among others, offer the promise of a complete answer. These systems can solve some problems but aren't always the flexible solution they need to be – and they can be overly complex to master.

Alternatively, there are other smaller digital tools and resources out there, ready to solve every problem you might have – plus a few you hadn't thought of yet! Room management help? There's an app for that. Reward badges? Plenty of those. What about a tool that offers a discussion space, mixed with a whiteboard, mixed with... well, there are also plenty of those.

Understanding the routines that are already present in your classroom is our first step to understanding how to best employ digital tools effectively, both in the physical classroom and in your online classroom.

After all, in most cases you don't need to adopt an entirely new practice in order to integrate technology. Often, you can transition many aspects of your existing classroom technique in a way that enriches and strengthens your current pedagogy.

Learning routines

Let's start to look at this more closely with an example of a common classroom thinking routine that many teachers employ habitually in their classrooms: Think-Pair-Share. This simple visible thinking routine is one that most teachers will be intimately familiar with in nearly all stages of a student's developmental path: asking students to reflect on their learning, pairing them up or putting them in small groups to further explore and reframe that knowledge and then drawing the whole class together to share and develop new understandings.

This simple routine promotes, supports and reveals the benefit of reframing knowledge for students and provides a vehicle to incorporate thinking language into the classroom, making the processes of the learning taking place explicit. As you transition through each phase of this routine, teacher observations guide the students towards an understanding of how and why the routine benefits their learning.

"As I'm walking around the room, I can hear some really interesting points of view based on your past experience, so let's come back together as a group and share what we have discovered so far."

As Perkins (2003) observes, making the learning visible in this way encourages "a focus on the establishment of structures that weave thinking into the fabric of the classroom and help to make the thinking of everyone in the classroom more visible and apparent".

In other words, by using Think-Pair-Share, and observing why you are shifting between each stage of this routine with your students, you are supporting this and other models of thinking.

Thinking routines like this one allow us to stop and consider our progress. They support critical thinking by helping us organise and make connections as we progress towards new understandings. We can more readily identify our progress and refine our thinking when we are given opportunities to pause and consider our next steps, and our past efforts.

By using a strategy like this with your students, you are also providing a model for dispositional development. The routine pivots the learner to have a disposition towards thinking about thinking, and promotes the notion that patterns of thinking have value (Perkins, Jay & Tishman 1993).

Blythe and Associates (2009) tell us that by employing a routine like this one, we are also allowing learners to demonstrate as well as construct understandings of a topic. This routine, like many others, supports the development of a better understanding of the content as well as the appreciation of the method of inquiry.

Your students need opportunities to understand specific ways of thinking as they develop as learners, and they need structures of thinking they can turn to and employ independently as they progress towards greater independence. Equally, as they move towards more significant challenges, they are best advantaged by being able to nominate the type of thinking they need to engage with when and where it's needed.

When asked to structure an approach to a project, for example, a group of students familiar with the types of routines they have followed in the classroom will be able to nominate which offers the most advantage.

This type of routine isn't the only one present in your classroom, of course. You likely have a host of other routines, some formal and some less formal, some explicit in making thinking visible and some more habitual. Either way, the best results often come from making your intentions for employing those practices clear, and ensuring student participation and awareness of their purpose is, well, routine.

As we work with young people, helping them to learn how to learn, routines provide structure and safety in our classrooms, and our routines are the framework within which learning often occurs.

Why digital tools are useful

In much the same way that routines support student learning and can help in their understanding of the ways in which thinking can be made visible and purposeful, students need to understand how and why the digital tools they are employing in the classroom are also useful.

With so much reflexive and unconscious use of technology in our lives, often occurring without critique or reflection, students need guidance to employ the technology around them with purpose and understanding.

Students are best advantaged when they are able to identify the specific digital tools most worthwhile in reaching the outcome they are in pursuit of.

If we are not explaining why we are using one digital tool over another, why one digital resource stands apart for the job before us, how can we expect students to come away from our classrooms armed with a critical view?

Knowing which digital tool to use and when offers students a significant advantage, not just in their schooling, but in later life. If they are able to critically evaluate the options and make a clear decision on how they might collaborate or share a resource, or perhaps even build a community, they are significantly advantaged.

Think-Pair-Share

Let us return to Think-Pair-Share for a moment.

You might begin this visible thinking routine by asking your students to quietly reflect and write down four key ideas related to a topic.

Be sure to offer students sufficient time to reflect. It's this part of the routine where they are not only recalling prior knowledge, but strengthening that knowledge drawn up from long-term memory.

You may then ask them to pair up and compare and contrast the ideas they created, reminding them that the purpose of sharing these perspectives is to gain a broader understanding of the topic, and to uncover what they already know and some of what they don't know.

Finally, you might bring students back into a group discussion, explaining that this will help to identify broad themes and common ideas that were raised.

Now, consider the same process, but replace one of these steps with a digital tool, a simple chat room, for example. Students are asked to reflect individually; you then ask them to discuss in an online chat room the ideas each of them has developed independently. You explain that the purpose of this transition is to share perspectives, and to ensure that everyone's contributions are valued as the transcript from each chat room will be shared once the chat has concluded.

You might also follow by asking students to *Add to* or *Build on* what's been contributed, or *Challenge* what was observed (ABC), further developing the contributions in the chat.

Bring your students back together, gather the transcripts of their discussions and ask them to rank the responses.

You can see that the difference between using a chat room and not using a chat room with the students in the Pair part of the routine is not a huge departure from your original approach. What has changed, however, is significant. The chat room allows for an assessable digital record to be kept of the discussion, and it also means that a detailed record of the ideas is available to aid in the class discussion that follows.

The transcript also presents a significant difference, in that every student contribution in the chat will be considered in the class discussion on its merits. Students that contribute ideas in the chat room that are missed or passed over too quickly will still see their ideas considered a second time in the whole-class discussion and ranking task. This encourages students engaged in an online discussion to move on confidently – it also allows the discussion to have the opportunity to deepen as students feel equally confident their ideas are and will be valued.

Most importantly, swapping this particular digital tool into your existing routine is also straightforward – if the chat room you used is simple to use and designed to do one thing, and to do it well, it's far more easily integrated quickly and simply into your routine.

Students have also, in this sequence of learning, been given something particularly useful. They have been made aware of the benefits of the pedagogical approach being employed and how it supports their learning, but they are also now better informed as to the real value of the use of the chat room in their learning and the consolidation of ideas.

When you explain the purpose and benefit of using a chat room for the discussion, they will, over time, appreciate future strategic use of that tool in and outside the classroom. They will also begin to appreciate the role they play in that online discussion, and how it befits the next activity.

The students' consideration of the value of a tool outside the classroom and how it might be considered in their own informal learning environments is also an important consideration. The line between formal and informal learning is notably diminishing. Informal learning environments are also considered to be particularly effective avenues for learning or, as Diana Laurillard (2018) puts it, a "powerful force for learning".

The need for young people to understand how and why to use the digital tools we employ could be argued as one that's increasingly important to inform not just what learning occurs in the classroom, but the learning they undertake with friends, in online discussions on the bus or exploring areas of interest at home.

Later in this book, we'll look more closely at how you can approach and articulate the benefits of digital tools to young adults.

It's also important at this juncture that I clarify that when I refer to a 'simple chat room', I'm talking about a chat space that is exactly as described: simple. It's a chat room that has few features and allows only for students to participate in discussion. Picture a chat room that does one thing well, online discussion, one that's quick to employ and devoid of any features not absolutely necessary. Why? Because when the use of this type of tool is clear, its purpose and function in this routine are also clear.

Mind-mapping

Let's look at another example.

A teacher enters her classroom and as is her common practice puts up the learning intention for that day on the board as the first order of business. With the purpose of the lesson established, she moves on, returning to the statement as the class progresses through the lesson.

However, replace the whiteboard comment with a simple no-frills, online mind-mapping resource – another simple tool – and the impact changes significantly. The learning intention becomes a more malleable object, and as the class progresses and the students make headway towards their goal, these successes can be recorded alongside the learning intention.

Again, at the transition between tools, between steps in a sequence of learning, the teacher should articulate the reasons for that transition and the use of the digital tool being employed. In this case, the teacher may say something such as, "We're going to look at our learning intentions for the day. We're using our mind-mapping tool to allow us to observe the intentions clearly, but also to allow us to change or expand upon those intentions over time, and to help us learn more about what we have understood."

Students can see the intention of their learning, and an outline of the scaffolding that took them there. They are able to develop ownership and participate in building out the sequence.

More than that, though, the students are, over time, encouraged to appreciate the specific benefit of the digital tool being employed for this purpose. Because the tool is clear in its purpose, the benefit of this digital resource in this sequence of learning is also made clearer.

Again, the tool was easily accommodated into an existing routine because the purpose of that digital tool was clear. With a strong understanding of the simple affordances that the tool offered, the teacher was able to embed it quickly and easily into the existing routine. The use of a digital tool in both examples promotes new understandings and connections as students move towards a broader goal. In the mind-mapping example, the learning intention has become something dynamic, engendering a sense of co-ownership and agency shared between educator and students. Weaker students will better understand the path they are taking; stronger students can consider alternate paths to success and witness milestones recorded as they move to new levels of understanding.

You might argue that a whiteboard would serve our purpose just as well, however, once you take account of the way in which this tool can be paired with other resources, its benefit becomes clear. If your mapping tool allows you to export the results as an image, for example, this can be quickly shared with the class and employed in a range of other digital resources. Cross-contextual use is therefore a key consideration in why you might reach for a digital tool in this instance.

Key takeaways

- Routines support student dispositional development promoting valued patterns of thinking.
- There's strong value in enhancing awareness of digital tool value – both formal and informal.
- Classroom routines, simple and complex, can be the framework for incorporating digital tools.
- Simple digital tools are easier to align with steps into these routines.

Sum it up

Pairing classroom routines with digital tools can improve the clarity of a pedagogical approach and allow students to more easily understand their purpose in a sequence of learning. Employing digital tools with a clear purpose, teachers and students can more easily appreciate their value and role.

CHAPTER 2

Establishing a foundation

One of the key benefits of using simple tools is our improved capacity to better illustrate and understand how and why technology is being employed in our own reflections and with students. It's through that clarity that we are increasingly able to appreciate how and why we might deepen our employment of technology use in the classroom.

This is perhaps best illustrated with the use of Dr Ruben Puentedura's SAMR model, which provides a framework to show the impact of technology on teaching and learning (Puentedura, 2013). Dr Puentedura may argue that using a digital tool as we've seen in the previous chapter has allowed us to modify the original routine and enrich student opportunities with our new approach. His work is often used as a guide when considering the depth of technology use and student achievement within a sequence of learning.

In our use of each new digital tool in our classrooms, SAMR supports our understanding of how and where we might consider a replacement of an existing step in our pedagogical approach with a digital tool, or where we might seek to redefine the task entirely through technology.

The SAMR Model (Dr Ruben R Puentedura)

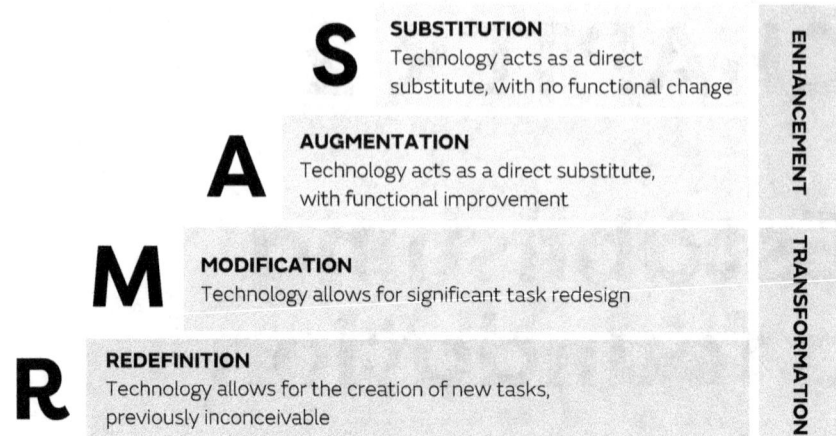

(Source: Wikimedia Commons)

SAMR is a spectrum, from simple Substitution with a digital resource to Augmentation through that tool of our original approach, through to Modification and a complete Redefinition of the task in a way only possible with technology. As we employ digital resources in our classrooms, the model invites us to consider how we are using technology to transform and extend learning experiences for students.

Often, SAMR is used to help us determine whether an enhancement or even a complete redefinition of a task is possible, but it also helps us to determine whether it is needful. It is a mistake to think that redefining every classroom routine through technology should be the goal. Sometimes, simply substituting a previous approach by incorporating technology is what's needed, or even what's ideal. Replacing a pedagogical step with an increasingly complex form of technology does not always result in a stronger outcome, nor should it always be our objective.

In some schools, SAMR is used at the **Substitution** or **Augmentation** phases, but rarely gets beyond these. This is often in part because the next steps towards deeper application are not sufficiently scaffolded for staff or students. In these school settings, the fault often lies with a lack of appropriate support or the provision of an appropriate framework to move to a more complex use of technology, towards modifying the approach or redefining the activity through technology.

Those steps towards increasingly sophisticated employment of technology can be challenging. This increased complexity in the classroom really is, in my experience, often where the art of our teaching practice meets the science.

By using digital tools with a clear purpose, you'll more readily be able to recognise opportunities for depth in their employment to technology in your classroom. Simple tools – digital tools that do one thing well – do not necessarily also equate to a simple application. The benefit of employing small, nimble, digital tools is that you can, as you gain confidence, use them in increasingly sophisticated combinations.

Digital resources with a clear purpose

Let's pause at this point and consider technology in the classroom, but from another perspective. Let's look at the tool first.

Consider the resources available to you when you set out to make an audio recording for your class – or hope to have the students record some audio. A tool we might reach for is Audacity, a freely available and powerful audio-recording tool.

The second tool we might consider is the audio recorder offered by voice-recorder-online.com. It's a simple and easy-to-use recording tool with one button to press. The audio quality isn't at the standard you might achieve with Audacity, but it's certainly good enough to allow a student to record an audio file in under a minute without having to download and install software, without having to log in – and, in fact, without any prior knowledge of audio at all.

Both are purposeful and powerful tools for use in the classroom. The first requires sophisticated knowledge of a myriad of features – Audacity is a notable piece of software that allows granular control and refinement of audio files.

If our focus was on creating perfect audio and developing a deeper understanding of the way in which audio recordings are best attained, it would perhaps be a good fit. It is, however, a scalpel and we only need a butter knife in this instance. The voice-recorder-online.com audio recorder allows anyone to record an audio file quickly with minimal fuss.

Time is a significant consideration in the classroom and students can create their audio file briskly using voice-recorder-online.com, allowing the teacher to use that audio file in a host of different ways in the classroom. Students might share them, rank them or build larger resources with them – there are endless possibilities.

As the voice-recorder-online.com recording tool is quick to master and easy to employ, the teacher can reach for it reflexively as the need arises – or use the tool in concert with others within a more complex sequence of learning with far fewer impediments.

In short, both tools are worthwhile, but the resource offered by voice-recorder-online.com allows a teacher and their students to employ it quickly and, as they gain confidence, to leverage the recorded audio in increasingly complex ways. Teachers using voice-recorder-online.com are advantaged using a digital tool with a clear purpose that's briskly understood by all involved.

Classrooms require a foundational approach to using technology, one that supports that further complexity. The key is understanding how your pedagogy, content and the technology are best aligned as you refine your practice.

As is often said about foundational skills, "you need to know the rules before you can break them". Simple tools give you this foundation, helping you – but also, critically – helping your students to understand more deeply how different digital tools can be employed and for what purpose. It doesn't replace the need for tools like Audacity, but recognises that often in the classroom, a digital tool with a clear purpose that's briskly applied with a minimum of effort is worth 10 Audacities!

Once you understand the deeper purpose and opportunities afforded by different types of technology in alignment with different pedagogical approaches, your opportunity to move beyond **Augmentation** and **Modification** in Dr Puentedura's SAMR model becomes more possible. You can reach greater complexity because you appreciate the deeper purpose and opportunity afforded by tools with a clear purpose.

The digital resources you employ should be clear in their purpose, and swift and straightforward to employ. In this way, you and your students can better understand the best digital tool for each part of the learning journey. As your students become more sophisticated in their use of combinations of digital tools to reach a learning outcome, your capacity and theirs to further augment and modify an approach becomes more feasible in a way that's sustainable and clearly understood by teacher and student.

As you move beyond **Substitution** and **Augmentation** in some tasks towards **Modification** and **Redefinition**, you are also shifting towards more strategic and extended thinking with students. Simple tools support the capacity of you and your students to recognise when and why you might make this shift.

Thinking routines

Routines can be a powerful strategy to employ when using simple tools, as they allow us to more easily recognise how and where technology might be used to best effect. When you are exploring ways in which you might redefine technology use in your classroom, they can be a great place to start that journey. Let's return to our routines for a moment to further clarify why this is important.

Sure, they are widely used, and they can make thinking more visible, but what else is there about thinking routines that benefits your students?

Critically, they employ repetition as a key characteristic, allowing them to be embedded deeply in your classroom. Regular use of thinking routines helps your students to develop a strong relationship with their purpose and place in developing new understandings. Well-established routines create predictability and a secure learning environment for learners at all levels and from a wide variety of backgrounds and experiences.

Your classroom routines help your students to reflect on and consolidate learning. Many thinking routines are also designed principally to help generate lots of ideas, and to allow students to reframe knowledge.

Thinking routines encourage students to look for comparisons and connections, empowering learners to look for evidence to support their own perspectives. They also empower educators to distribute responsibility for learning evenly across all participants in the classroom.

What makes effective routines stand apart? An effective routine will encourage your students to ask questions and explore ideas from multiple perspectives. Good thinking routines wrap significant research up into a simply understood pattern of thinking – simple enough to grasp quickly, but a way of thinking that guides student efforts in more complex ways.

All learning sequences are patterns or actions of behaviour (Ritchhart, Church & Morrison, 2011). They help us to chunk and automate information, to make our thinking more evident to us as we progress. They can also more readily support the transition of new ideas and new knowledge to long-term memory as we organise and consolidate our understandings through the routine.

What follows below is a summary of some of the more commonly known 'core' classroom routines, and a brief description of each. These routines are accompanied by descriptions of the sorts of cognitive behaviours that the routines encourage.

Think-Puzzle-Explore

This routine encourages students to identify their prior knowledge. It's also helpful in guiding them towards new ideas and helps to lay the groundwork for their own inquiry on a particular subject. It's best used at the start of a project. Students begin by identifying what they already know about a topic and then generate questions, things that 'puzzle' them, or problems to resolve. The exploration phase encourages students to identify or construct and carry out a method to answer those questions.

I used to think, now I think

This routine is one many of you will be familiar with and is best employed as a way of helping students to connect with why their knowledge and understanding around a topic have changed. It is also a way of consolidating ideas on a subject and tracking learning growth.

See-Think-Wonder

This routine guides your students towards more thoughtful observations when confronted with a new topic or idea, work completed by their peers or a piece of art – it's very adaptable! What do they see? What do they think? What do they wonder about? It fosters curiosity and encourages interpretation, opening a pathway into open-ended inquiry.

Think-Pair-Share

This routine is widely known and used – it might even perhaps be considered critical to the profession! Think-Pair-Share is often employed to encourage students to consider multiple perspectives, and to help consolidate emergent ideas on a topic.

Generate-Sort-Connect-Elaborate

This routine supports students' activation of prior knowledge, guiding them towards the creation of new ideas. It helps students to connect and consolidate their thinking. It's also helpful as a way of guiding students towards reflections on the direction their thinking has taken them around a particular subject or idea. Concept mapping, where connections are made between ideas, is a common method of executing this routine.

Colour-Symbol-Image

This routine guides students towards identifying the 'essence' of a particular concept. It's designed to encourage them to use multiple forms of reflection when they take on new ideas, and to express abstract ideas in a concrete form.

Other common thinking routines

There are countless thinking routines you might reach for, in part because of the myriad of combinations you might also elect to use. Those outlined above are simply the ones considered more commonly used and that target different types of thinking across a spectrum of routines you might employ. You are very likely to have less-formal routines you employ as well, those you've developed over time that work well in your classroom with your students.

There are some other benefits to embracing routines more broadly within a school. They provide a common language for teachers that encourage a common instructional language. Routines can often be employed across disciplines and can encourage teachers to compare a more granular understanding of practice.

The depth of use of thinking routines is beyond the scope of this book, but if you're keen to explore the subject further, I recommend the Project Zero Thinking Routine Toolbox (pz.harvard.edu/thinking-routines). This is a fantastic resource provided by Harvard Graduate School and is well worth exploring. I also recommend *Making Thinking Visible* by Ron Ritchhart as a wonderful resource exploring research-based approaches to teaching thinking strategies. See the references at the back of this book for full details of both resources.

ACTIVITY 1

Work template: This book includes several activities that link together to form one longer iterative reflection. As you complete each one, you'll slowly build your awareness of the thinking routines you already engage in and how they align with simple digital tools in sequences of learning that support your practice.

In this first activity, we're going to identify the routines in your classroom.

Try to identify the features of some of your classroom thinking routines and tease out each separate stage within them. I've started you off with a few examples.

Title	Step 1	Step 2	Step 3	Step 4
Welcome	Greet students at the door	Call them by name	Personal anecdote	Reflection on class values
Reflection	Contributions of two things they understood	Two concerns that still remain	Two things they'd like to pursue further	Links to the new lesson and Learning Intentions
Pre-reading link	Write the Learning Intentions on the board	Discuss pre-reading	Pair and discuss	Whole-class discussion
Think-Pair-Share	Independent reflection	Paired shared reflection	Group discussion	Check for understanding

You can see from my examples above that in this exercise the routine you outline doesn't have to be complex. What's important is to consider all the components of each step in the routine.

We'll use these reflections in the chapters that follow.

Interaction phases

There are many common phases of interaction in routines, with five that are common among core routines. These are discussion, mapping, sequencing, connection and reflection.

Identifying phases that are common within the routines you use can help to identify the key purpose of the digital tool you're employing. Of course, these particular five phases are not the only ones that can be observed in a great variety of thinking routines and other classroom routines, but they are some of the more common ones, and a great place to start!

I've identified these in five phases partly because of their commonality, but also because of the frequency in which we see these types of interactions working fluidly together. Classroom discussion is often accompanied by connection and reflection. Sequencing ideas is frequently accompanied by an activity that involves reflection or further connection and development.

We'll look at each of these phases in more detail in chapters 6 and 7.

ACTIVITY 2

Next, we're going to identify the phases present in the routines you've already identified in your classroom. Against each of your routines, consider the types of interaction that might be most appropriately matched. Place against your own routines, the types of interactions most appropriate. You might consider whether some of those mentioned earlier are relevant to the routines you have identified: discussion, mapping, sequencing, connection and reflection.

You may choose to simply leave some phases blank, recognising that for those parts of your routine, you'd prefer to keep that interaction offline.

Title	Step 1	Step 2	Step 3	Step 4
Reflection	Contributions of two things they understood	Two concerns that still remain	Two things they'd like to pursue further	Links to the new lesson and Learning Intentions
Phases	**Reflection**		**Mapping**	
Pre-reading link	Write the Learning Intentions on the board	Discuss pre-reading	Pair and discuss	Whole-class discussion
Phases	**Mapping**	**Reflection**	**Connection**	**Sequencing**
Think-Pair-Share	Independent reflection	Paired shared reflection	Group discussion	Check for understanding
Phases	**Reflection**	**Discussion**		**Sequencing**

Establishing a foundation 27

Key takeaways

- Simple tools with a clear purpose allow teachers to more easily recognise opportunities for depth and sophistication in digital tool use.
- Routines offer the benefit of a common language, exposing the method and virtue of visible thinking, which aligns with the clear purpose and application of digital tools.
- Discussion, mapping, sequencing, connection and reflection are common interactions frequently employed within thinking routines.

Sum it up

Many classroom routines include common interactions and by recognising them, we can more easily align them with a digital tool's purpose that further facilitates depth and clarity of application.

Put it into action

Consider what other routines you're aware of that are employed by your colleagues in their classrooms. Pick one and evaluate it in terms of the different phases within the routine, and with consideration of how you might adapt it for your own classroom.

CHAPTER 3

Finding simple tools

We've identified some of the routines you're familiar with and perhaps you've identified a few new ones you're keen to try. We've also identified some of the interactions that we feel are appropriate and commonly seen in phases of our classroom routines.

In this chapter, we'll turn our attention to the types of digital tools we might be using to achieve each step in a routine. We'll clarify the features you should look for to more easily identify an appropriate digital tool for your classroom, and the design elements common to resources you might seek out.

There are countless digital resources for classrooms available, but many are simply not designed for use in F-12 classrooms. It's easy to see why teachers become frustrated by the choices they are presented with or obliged to use. It seems as though at every conference, every session of professional development and every education trade show, there is an endless sea of digital resources demanding our attention.

What follows is a way of looking at digital classroom resources that cuts through the hype and bluster, to help you find tools that are fit for your purpose and your students.

The myth that young adults are intuitively good users of technology is not only misguided, but disenfranchises those students in the classroom that do not have the technical skills to participate. Present them with complex software or a poorly designed interface and they are often more likely than many adults to struggle and disengage.

Pew Research Center findings support this, recognising that with young adults, "frequent exposure to computers and the internet makes them very comfortable around digital scenes, but their actual technical skill and understanding is poor when compared with their adult counterparts" (Anderson & Perrin, 2017).

There's a good reason this book is called *Simple Tools*. I suggest that digital tools that do one thing simply and do it well are often worth a dozen more complex digital classroom resources. Online tools that are clear in purpose and design are far more adaptable to classroom routines and more readily explained to and accommodated by young adults. Simple tools that do one thing and do it well can also serve to encourage young people to have a more thoughtful and purposeful use of the huge array of technology that surrounds them.

Time and big platforms

Michael Barbour tells us that a strong knowledge of digital platforms is a key ingredient needed in the capacity of teachers to teach effectively in online spaces. This is particularly true for many large learning platforms, where to understand how to effectively teach within them, you need to have a deep knowledge of the options that sit beneath each activity type.

Teachers are by far the busiest people I know. The time needed to understand how to best leverage deep features in a learning platform is time we often simply don't have. Simple tools provide an answer – with the use of nimble digital resources that fit neatly within your sequence of learning – tools that allow you to more clearly understand their application and purpose, and enable you to shift more briskly to an alternate approach when the need arises.

Of course, this isn't true for all large learning platforms. Not all digital platforms are created equal! Some, like the Google for Education suite, have a lower bar to access and include resources like Jamboard that are simple for students to quickly master.

Stile is another platform that offers accessible features and notable flexibility in an application linked explicitly to the curriculum. Teachers using Stile still need to have a deeper knowledge of the broader systems than the Simple Tools approach suggests; however, time is saved elsewhere in planning and preparation.

At the heart of good teaching practice lies the simple truth that teachers need to clearly understand how to best match the right digital tool with the most appropriate pedagogical approach and content that's suited to that approach and environment.

Some large platforms are moving towards designs that allow this to be achieved more easily. My approach doesn't lock out those platforms. Instead, it gives you a way of discerning the right digital tool for the job, a way of recognising those digital tools that are cumbersome, not fit for purpose and not designed well enough for classroom use!

Regardless of whether or not you're using a large platform, stuck in a walled garden or using a blend of different tools and approaches, or simply don't know where to start, use the checklist that appears on page 40 to examine what makes good digital tools great in the classroom.

At the end of the next section, you'll then be encouraged to reflect upon how well the digital resources you currently use stack up. I'd suggest having a few in your mind that you find challenging to employ with students, as you read through this next section.

What does a simple digital tool look like? What should we look for as teachers as we compare the myriad of different options out there?

Barbour and Adelstein's work (2013) tells us that what young people want from learning spaces online are tools that are purposeful and useful. As we guide young people from task to task, from one metacognitive understanding to the next, students need the same clarity around the digital tools they are employing as they do around the purpose behind the learning strategy being used. They need to know when they recognise the need to collaborate, which approach is best and which digital tool may be best suited to that purpose. Let's look at some examples of tools that meet that need.

Tlk.io

Tlk.io is a chat room with a clean design and a great deal of empty space that helps to emphasise what's important. While there are some sponsorship logos on the front page, none are animated and they are limited to that page, so any possible distraction that might cause for students is kept to a minimum.

To create a chat room, you simply come up with a chat room name and enter it when prompted. You now have a simple chat room with a web address that's easily shared.

Best of all, the chat room is simple to use. You place your name in the box when prompted and join the discussion. Tlk.io lacks a range of features offered by other chat rooms and therein lies the advantage: there's nothing to distract you, nothing to draw you away from the discussion.

It also allows you to set up a chat space quickly and easily. It does one thing and it does it well – and because of that and its clean design and simple affordances, it is a perfect tool to dynamically switch to when the need arises.

To use a more complex discussion portal, you'd very likely have to prepare your students in advance. You might have to talk them through registration and provide them with instructions on the features and how to employ them. You'd need to be prepared for possible distractions and diversions due to advertising or the breadth of unrelated features and resources it promotes – these will likely distract your students from the activity at hand.

Tlk.io cuts through all of those concerns by doing only chat – and doing it well. It's quick to set up and equally quick to master. You can have a class set up with multiple chat spaces inside five minutes and can focus on the discussion and its purpose. Because of the ease of use, clear purpose and simple design, it's also easy to shift to from tlk.io to just about any other digital resource.

Mind maps

Let's look at another example, mindmaps.app. The first thing you'll notice about this tool is that you're able to make a brisk start without logging in.

Mindmaps.app does offer saving options and account creation, but this doesn't stand in the way of you making a quick start.

Saving

Not saving does come with risks, no question. Power outage? Internet dropout? You may lose what work you've started. The question comes down to the purpose of your use of the resource. If your intent is to ask students to create work that they return to and build on over time, then an option that has login as a first step to access is likely more needful.

If, however, your intent is to use the tool quickly in a sequence of learning, then mindmaps.app may well be a preferred option. Having a mapping tool that can be drawn on quickly in a sequence of learning has notable advantages.

There are a range of more complex features available if you dig for them, but the clean design and clearly considered purpose of this resource mean that your first and most strongly encouraged action is to start your mind map. As you work on it, developing your ideas, further features become slowly evident.

Mindmaps.app isn't trying to be anything other than a solid option for mind mapping – and it shows. The clean design, straightforward range of resources and brisk set-up means you can have students mind mapping in the classroom in mere minutes. Want students to use it as a precursor to chat online? Great! Pair it with tlk.io and make it the stimulus for a broader discussion.

The 'Think' element of your Think-Pair-Share routine might become:

> **Think:** Ask students to open up a mind map and brainstorm on the topic you're exploring that day in class. Students can save the results of their work as a PNG file with a couple of quick clicks.
>
> **Pair:** Set students together to discuss the merits of the ideas presented, then record the ideas discussed in a chat room using tlk.io. The use of the chat room transcript is a perfect way to transition into the final part of your routine.
>
> **Share:** You now have a record of the discussion and ideas ready to be ranked, sequenced, cut up and distributed or even printed and sorted by students at home or in the classroom. You also have a wonderful record of the learning sequence, and the efforts of the class that you can employ in assessment.

Using simple tools – straightforwardly designed digital tools – you're able to move swiftly between these different interactions in a way that wastes little time and maximises the opportunity for students to appreciate the purpose behind the transitions.

In much the same way that you might reflect upon the transitions in Think-Pair-Share with your students, you'll want to do the same with these digital tools.

For example, you might begin by explaining the benefit of using a mind map, that these tools support students in the clarifying and expanding upon the connections between ideas. You may also consider talking about them as a way of sharing ideas without evaluating them. When moving on to your use of tlk.io, you might explain the value of using a chat room rather than paired face-to-face discussion, as it will allow you to take advantage of the transcripts later and encourages students to reflect and consider their contribution more carefully.

Tool choice

How do we choose the right digital tools that have a low cognitive burden, and that more readily allow for swift transitions in the classroom as we move through a sequence of learning? We need to understand what design elements make them simple!

What follows are some considerations to guide you in your search.

Ease of use

The resource must have a clear purpose with a clean and easily understood design. The research is clear on this point, with 'ease of use' directly linked to the more likely adoption of classroom tools (Davis, 1989; Venkatesh & Davis, 2000). The greater the complexity of the tool and the more features offered, the more information a student may consider within their working memory as they use that tool.

The greater the extraneous load set aside to grasp the use of a digital tool, the less that's available for the actual problem your students are working on. Another way to think about it is to consider the digital tool in a similar way that you might a student's study space at home. If the workspace is clear of distractions and only has the tools they need, it's more straightforward to approach the work ahead. If the study space is messy, with unnecessary distractions cluttering up the place, it's harder to focus on the task at hand.

Quick mastery

Digital tools need to be quick to grasp. You don't want to have to waste significant time getting everyone comfortable with a new digital resource; you want to move straight to the activity you had planned and focus on the type of interaction you'd like to see in that phase of your learning sequence, confident that students can employ the digital resource quickly and easily.

Singular purpose

Your new digital classroom tools should be great at doing one thing really well. Tools that are goal-driven, that do one thing and provide a focus on performing that task effectively, are simpler to employ and easier to master.

These types of tools are also quicker to differentiate with, as they allow you to employ them more easily and explicitly with students, regardless of their prior experience.

Access constraints

Digital tools in the classroom that don't demand complex login details or require lengthy setting up allow you to employ them briskly. Incorrect passwords, complex registration requirements and forgotten usernames can all mean delays and distractions. While there are advantages to having accounts – the Google tool suite is a good example of an exception to this rule – not having to register an account simplifies your approach in the classroom.

If a digital tool is browser-based and requires no login (you can simply use the digital tool in your web browser), that's a huge advantage in getting started quickly with a new resource. Leaning towards a suite of digital tools that all employ a Google sign-in is another example of the way in which you might avoid any additional unnecessary complexity.

There are some wonderful simple tools you can download onto laptops in the classroom, and you shouldn't discount them by any means, but occasional tool updates, installation help with new laptops, etc, all create delays and distraction. If you can find a browser-based version, my advice is to lean towards that resource instead.

Integrations

Of course, if you are a Google or Microsoft school, you may feel differently about access constraints, and that's fine, too! There's a good deal to be gained from having a single sign-in option for the software you employ. Leaning heavily towards tools that allow you to use a Google login, for example, can simplify storage and the sharing of resources. You'll also increase the options available to you if you broaden your search of digital tools to include resources that may require a Google login, for example.

In my experience, often those deeper integrations do also come with their own complexities, and a cost/benefit assessment must be closely considered. For example, how and with whom you share your files and what privileges you allow them can add some complexity when using the Google product range.

My advice? Keep your eye on the design and access benefits of the resources you consider. Keep it simple, and if you are inclined to use a resource that requires a single sign-on, balance the access advantages against further complexity that it may introduce.

The purpose of taking on an approach like Simple Tools is to strip back the complexity and focus on the purpose of the digital tool within a sequence of learning. If you feel that a slightly more complex tool is worth the additional complications, pay close attention when you employ it to determine whether the cost is ultimately worthwhile.

Minimal and accessible language

Ensure the vocabulary used in the tool is approachable for your audience and check that phrases and concepts are familiar to your students. As an example, some chat rooms might mention branching discussions. Many students would need support to understand how this relates to their contribution. When less than 90-95% of the vocabulary students are presented with when contending with a problem is unknown, studies suggest their comprehension of the task is severely diminished. The same impact might be anticipated in the employment of a digital tool, where language used within it is less clearly understood.

A clean and minimalist design is perhaps the simplest indication of a tool designed for ease of use. Look for oceans of white space, minimal text or none at all where possible. When each new feature on the page competes for your students' attention, particularly in the early stages of their adoption, less is more.

Digital tool design

There are also some design heuristics that can further support your choice of digital tool and that underpin some of the advice given above. I've drawn particularly on Nielsen and Molich's work in my selection of heuristics aligned with this purpose. Note that this is not a finite list and there are other functions you might look to for a specific task that calls on particular features.

Is there an undo button? If the student makes a mistake, is it a simple matter to step back and correct the error? This also depends, of course, on whether mistakes are seen in the context of your sequence of learning as an opportunity or an impediment.

Are there too many instructions? Is there anything that is not immediately obvious to you in the design? If you can't quickly and intuitively recognise the purpose of buttons or directions, then expect a portion of your student cohort to be equally confused. Your digital tool design will ideally rely on an intuitive recognition of the right path rather than forcing you to recall which steps to follow and when.

Can you check for understanding? Barbour and Adelstein's work with F-12 students (2013) also suggests that students look for digital tools that help them check their understandings, keep them on track and reinforce their learning.

By employing tools that are simple in design and clear in their purpose, students have greater clarity in which tools are – or should be – used and why. This helps to continually reinforce the relevance of the tool and the work they are undertaking.

Because these types of tools are brisk to employ, further transitions are possible within a learning sequence during a single lesson, supporting frequent reflection and ongoing assessment. This frequent interactivity also allows for a more complex application in the use of the digital tools within a learning sequence.

What digital resources are out there that meet the Simple Tools requirements? There are literally hundreds, thousands! Selecting resources by recommendation is an obvious place to begin, enabling you to opt for something that has already been tested in a classroom. Where that isn't possible or you are seeking an alternative, this book offers direction when appraising what is available.

As we reflect again on Nielsen's work, we know that an online resource must enable the user 'to perform useful tasks'. That seems logical, but in practice many websites offer options that simply aren't required for the job at hand, or with a classroom in mind.

The simple fact is that many digital tools we employ in our classrooms were not designed with our classroom in mind but developed for larger markets and business settings. Like many theories employed in education, many of the tools we employ in the classroom also started with a boardroom or office in mind rather than a classroom.

Simplicity, in terms of the resource design at least, is what I strive to uncover whenever I am looking for a new online tool to use with students. Being specific about the sorts of outcomes you're striving for with your students will also narrow the field considerably. Thinking about the phases of interaction we explored earlier, consider as part of your classroom routine what essential function the tool needs to serve.

ACTIVITY 1

In this activity, we're going to use some of the design features common to simple tools and rank the resources you already use with your students. Use the IMPACT checklist below to determine how well the resources you currently use stack up. I'd suggest using this table to assess several resources, and at least one that you're unfamiliar with.

Checklist

Use the 1 to 5 score on the right in the table below, where 1 indicates very little concern and 5 indicates notable concern. Remember that the score YOU give a tool is subjective to your preferences and experience.

Simple tools have IMPACT		Score
IMPACT	**Have a clean intuitive design** Are there oceans of white space? Is the tool intuitive to navigate?	
MASTERY	**Allow quick mastery** With little prior knowledge, can you make an immediate start?	
PURPOSE	**Have a singular purpose** Does the tool do one thing well?	
ACCESS	**Have few access constraints** Can you access the tool without logging in or with minimal fuss?	
CONTEXT	**Supports cross-contextual use** Does it accommodate transitions to and from other digital tools?	
TEXT	**Have minimal text and accessible language** Is the text clear and concise, offering no hurdles to engagement?	

Consider the needs and capabilities of your young learners as you reflect upon the tools you use. Simonson, Schlosser and Orellana (2011) tell us to select tools that ask us to consider their needs and capabilities as we discern the right digital resource.

Are the tools you're currently employing well matched to the needs and capacity of the students you work with based on your new understanding of what constitutes an effective tool?

You may also wish to use the same activity with your students, asking them to consider how they might rank tools that are commonly known to them. Ask them which tools they prefer and why, which resources they are forced to use and how well suited they feel they are to the tasks they are set.

For example, you might ask your students to reflect upon the communication tools they use within the school that they are obliged to use. If you are a school that uses Microsoft Teams, how well does it stack up against the above digital tools design checklist, for example? What perspectives are commonly held by the students in your class around the use of that tool?

The purpose of the activity is to start developing an eye for what is more likely to work well in your classroom, and to allow you the opportunity to more critically evaluate current and future digital tools.

Student assessment

How you will assess and determine the learning needs of your students with a digital tool is an important consideration. There are a few things to bear in mind as you ascertain how easily you'll be able to use the student work in that digital tool to assess their capabilities:

- Will you use student work in this tool for assessment or will that occur in a latter part of your learning sequence?

- Is the intended assessment observational? If so, are you able to observe the student work without traversing the classroom? For example, can you ask for a link to their work that allows you to observe their use of the tool? Tlk.io is a good example of this, where once the chat rooms are up and running, getting access to simply named chat rooms is quick and easy.

- Does your digital tool enable ease of use for students with different contextual needs? Does it enable you to swiftly transition to and from that digital tool in your classroom from other resources? Look for digital resources that are quickly accessible, and that allow you to briskly download or print a copy of work in commonly recognisable formats that are easily employed in other parts of a learning sequence.

Key takeaways

- Not all digital tools are created equal; tools that do one thing and do it well with a clear purpose and design are more easily aligned with routines.

- Simple tools can exist independently or as part of larger platforms.

- There are design traits that allow us to more easily recognise what might be considered a 'simple tool'.

- Students benefit from digital tools that allow them to clarify their purpose, check for understanding and reinforce their learning.

Sum it up

Simple tools have common design features that promote ease of use, clear recognition of purpose and align more easily with classroom routines and sequence of learning. These tools also benefit students and teachers through a clarity of purpose and metacognitive explicitly.

Put it into action

Explore experimenting with new simple tools that meet the criteria in this chapter.

Reach out to colleagues to find out what digital tools they are employing and whether the criteria above are among their considerations when selecting those tools.

Observe the types of digital tools your students lean towards. Canvas them in terms of what they consider to be worthwhile or helpful features in the digital tools they use at school and in their own pursuits outside the classroom.

Use IMPACT to support your assessment of new digital resources in your classroom.

CHAPTER 4
Judging the load

There is little doubt in my mind that cognitive load and its impact on student learning in the classroom is one of the most important considerations we must contend with as teachers.

Cognitive load theory uses knowledge of the human brain to design teaching strategies that will maximise learning. Cognitive load is a critical consideration when determining a sequence of learning employing digital tools. Understanding how students best learn and why digital tool design can have an impact is a considerable advantage for every teacher.

In this chapter we'll explore some of the theory and align it with the ways in which simple tools can benefit learning in your classroom.

Digital resources designed for our classrooms and that are adaptive enough to support our students with a range cognitive, social and emotional needs can be a joy to work with. Poorly designed classroom tools can be an imposition at best and impede learning or worse – denigrate the benefit of digital tools for learning more broadly. The environment in which we work matters and the digital tools we use matter.

One of the key influences in the use of digital tools is their impact on our capacity to focus on the task at hand. Well-designed digital tools can do some of the work of memory for us, retaining our attention, ensuring our focus on the problem is balanced and considered. Well-considered digital tools can allow us to reach more deeply and with a clearer sense of their purpose within a learning sequence. Poorly designed digital tools, those overburdened by distraction and poor design can provide notable imposition on a student's capacity to engage with the task at hand.

New information takes up far more space in our working memory (Sweller, Ayres & Kalyuga, 2011), and so when working with new knowledge and new ideas, it's critical that we have a working environment that does not add further burden upon our working memory.

The impact of extraneous information – of unrelated information that's held in working memory – can have a dramatic influence over whether we are in a position to capably attend to a problem. Poorly designed tools, digital tools with complex navigation or that were designed to direct us towards outcomes other than the ones we're seeking, only add to existing cognitive burden as we attempt to understand and resolve a problem.

The limits of working memory

There's only so much we can hold in our working memory at any one time. As Lovell observes on Sweller's work, "For any learning to take place, a number of elements of new information must be considered and related in working memory, and then incorporated into long-term memory."

Working memory is limited both in duration and capacity when it is having to contend with new or 'novel' information. "The more elements of new information that a student is required to think about – to process in their working memory – during a learning task, and the more complex the relations between these elements – the number of interactions – the more challenging the learning task will be" (Lovell, 2020).

We can only hold and process a limited amount of novel information in our working memory at any one time. With a task set before students in the classroom, the more unnecessary information they have to contend with, the less available working memory remains to actually wrestle with the problem.

Our goal is to help students in their development of long-term memories that guide their thinking and understanding – memories that are well structured and durable (Mccrea, 2017).

Sweller contends that once information has been processed in working memory and stored as new knowledge in our long-term memory, it is then available to govern further action. It is this transference that is so fundamental to our work as teachers. There are no known limits when dealing with information drawn from long-term memory. The transformational effect of education is a consequence of our understanding of this process. With new knowledge in long-term memory, we can accomplish things we might not otherwise dream of achieving.

Extraneous load

This is the information that is unrelated to the problem at hand. Extraneous load is the term used to describe the distractions that impede our working memory from processing new information. This is the stuff that gets in the way of shifting new information into long-term memory. The more we can reduce extraneous load, the greater the amount of working memory available to us to solve the problem.

It could be a physical distraction in the classroom that is drawing student attention away, unrelated information that you've presented along with the key information for the task. It might also be the digital tools you're using to work through the problem. Digital tools that contain advertising features may cause a distraction or elements that are unnecessary to resolve the work students are undertaking.

Intrinsic load

This is the term used to describe the information required to resolve a problem. It is essentially the cognitive resources you need to shift new knowledge from your working memory to long-term memory. We want the working memory resources to be wholly focused on the problem we're trying to understand, with only the essential information that relates to the task taking up room in our working memory.

Our intrinsic load is influenced by how well it leverages our existing knowledge, how much new knowledge is required, and the number and degree of complexity in the interactions of those intrinsic elements required to solve the problem.

Well-designed sequences of learning seek to minimise the extraneous load elements and optimise intrinsic load. As Lovell observes, "Extraneous interacting elements are minimised through good instructional design" (Lovell, 2020). Use the right tools with a minimal amount of distraction and you set the scene for a working environment optimal to the right conditions needed. Simple digital tools allow us to further reduce the extraneous load and increase the likelihood of an optimal environment for learning.

Duration

The length of time students spend with a problem is critical to their capacity to understand and apply new knowledge and skills. When employing cumbersome or poorly designed digital tools, we can encounter delays in the establishment of the learning task, throughout the activity and in concluding and saving work.

At each of these three stages, delays impact heavily on the capacity of the student to respond to a problem and reflect on their efforts. A delay strains our intrinsic load and can frustrate our transition to the next scaffolded task. The longer we wait, the longer the delay from one stage of learning to the next, the harder it is to retain the information understood from the previous problem in our working memory.

To put it another way, let's say you've used a worked example with students to show them what success looks like for a particular problem. Great – this is a powerful and essential approach that has a high effect rating (Hattie, 2009) and a high rate of success in cognitive load theory (Sweller, Ayres & Kalyuga, 2011).

We know from Sweller's work that the longer you delay between a short and targeted discussion of an approach employed by an expert to the student's own opportunity to attempt to replicate the approach, the less likely the student will be able to find success. This is simply because of the delay between example and execution, between being given the essential information that relates to a successful approach and putting it into practice.

Introduce further delays in this process through the employment of poorly designed digital tools and your likelihood of success for students is further diminished.

Some of these delays could be, but are not limited to:

> **Login problems** and waiting for the class to be ready at the same time or delaying the application of instruction just given by the teacher and the students being ready and prepared to begin the work.
>
> **Tool complexity** is when digital tools simply offer many more features than are needed for the task at hand. I've often seen this to be the case with discussion tools, such as chat rooms or forum spaces. Complexity in both design and a myriad of features that simply aren't necessary to host the conversation results in an unnecessary range of choices being pressed upon students that distract them from the core work being undertaken.
>
> **Advertising and elements designed to distract** are a consideration here, and when promotional features are working hard to draw the attention of the learner, is it any wonder that their capacity to focus on the task is diminished? This isn't only limited to advertising for other services external to the tool, but internal promotion of features or paid services that have just as significant an impact upon the intrinsic load available to the student to complete the work. This can also take the form of elements included on a page to draw attention, but that are unrelated to the task at hand. A picture intended to get your attention, for example, but that has no purposeful link to the learning activity being presented can do more harm than good. Students might spend precious moments assessing the relationship between the image and the task, clarifying how or why it is related to the problem they are faced with.

Broad design concerns can often cause a delay or a distraction for students attempting to engage with a task where the activity demands a fraction of the features available or offers options useful only to an expert practitioner but that are unnecessary for the classroom. This isn't to say that there isn't a place for these types of complex tools, but when those additional features are not required and provide a distraction from the core task, they are an impediment. A broad array of text mark-up features in a chat room, for example, can add clarity and depth to a response, but where the purpose is to quickly glean student understanding on a topic, they can cause an unnecessary distraction.

Working memory

We can only hold so much information in our working memory at a time. In fact, when we're working on a problem, our working memory can generally contend with as few as three or four different interacting elements at any one time (though there is some contention around this number, given the range of influences that may affect our capacity and the decay of memory under an array of differing environments).

As we strive to focus our attention on a problem, we determine our focus on the elements we feel we will need to hold in our working memory. As we hold those ideas in our working memory and then attempt to elaborate on them, we draw on our long-term memories as a reference point that will allow us to make sense of them. As we juggle these multiple components, any extraneous load or burden that reduces the number of ideas in play reduces our overall capacity.

Mccrea observes that, "Good teachers don't just manage what students do in the classroom, they manage what they think. Because what students think about is ultimately what they learn" (Mccrea, 2017). Digital tools can be a notable aid in our efforts to more deeply understand complex issues or to resolve complex problems. However, if the digital tools we use are overburdened with unnecessarily complex navigational elements or by poor design, or contain unnecessary features or complexity, they inevitably demand our attending in unnecessary ways.

When we use tools with a clear purpose that do one thing well, we improve the likelihood of increasing the available memory we need to dedicate to the problem at hand.

Domain-general skills

"Domain-general skills refer to general capabilities that are applicable, and widely transferable, across a broad range of tasks. The teaching of '21st-Century Skills' or 'Enterprise Skills' – such as problem-solving, creativity, communication, teamwork and critical thinking – is founded on the assumption that these 'domain-general' skills exist, and can be taught, learned and transferred" (Lovell, 2020).

Using the Simple Tools approach, we can select digital tools that are simple in design and use them in classroom routines to achieve increasingly complex outcomes for students. This is also a method of supporting students to develop domain-general skills, that is, skills that are adaptable in a range of settings and that can underpin learning approaches that are not domain-specific.

There is another reason to give consideration to training students in domain-general skills, as these are the skills indelibly linked to the future careers of your students.

Creativity, problem-solving, teamwork, design and entrepreneurial skills – or what some call enterprise 21st-century or employability skills – are all demanded by employers. These skills are applicable to a broad range of careers and increasingly companies are looking for these skills ahead of more traditional qualifications.

Being able to respond to problems adaptably, to employ an enterprise skill set to new problems and to reflect effectively are skills vital to the employability of our young people.

There is another reason, however, that the Simple Tools approach supports the acquisition of these more flexible and adaptable skill sets, and that is that it supports our capacity to respond to failure.

By employing an iterative approach with young people to their employment of digital tools, by encouraging them to repeatedly reflect on the purpose and suitability of a tool for a task, students are more emboldened to contend with failure. We fail all the time, and it is our capacity to respond with a subset of skills that allow us to reflect and resiliently respond with purpose that enables progress.

It is through those repeated failures and our structured and reflective response to them that we build resilience and, perhaps, the grit to bounce back and find future success.

Digital tools and student success

The digital tools we use in the classroom should not overburden us with complexity, provide further barriers to learning or be unclear in their metacognitive benefit. Classroom tools should be clear in purpose and understood by students in a way that supports them to appreciate how else those tools might be employed in a variety of settings, not just in the classroom, but in their lives beyond it.

With a stronger appreciation for what constitutes design features that support the simple tools approach from the previous chapter, we might also now add four additional measures for success. These additional items are key considerations of simple tools design that influence the demand on a student's working memory and reduce the impact of unnecessary extraneous load.

> **Elements** – the number of elements present within the digital tool that the student must consider as they determine which features are relevant to the problem at hand.
>
> **Interactivity** – how much the digital tool demands of our working memory is also influenced by the degree of interactivity required to contend with in the problem at hand. For example, a contribution to a branching conversation in a forum may require consideration for the previous contributions first. A contribution to a discussion forum that allows only an independent contribution from each student, one that does not relate to previous entries, requires less interactivity and has a lower demand on working memory.

Independence – how autonomous our students are able to be in work that employs a digital tool.

Speed of application – how briskly students are able to apply the digital resource as they work towards a resolution of the problem.

If a digital tool is only as complex as it needs to be within the demanded context of the work at hand, the student is advantaged. If it demands less of our limited amount of working memory and if it offers the student the opportunity to get started quickly without support, then the student is advantaged. And if the student has a range of simple digital tools at their disposal, and they appreciate how they can be leveraged effectively when presented with new problems, they are further advantaged.

Key takeaways

- Teachers must take account of extraneous and intrinsic load in their creation of a sequence of learning with digital tools.
- Complex tools can add to a student's cognitive burden when confronting a problem.
- Digital tools that are complex can demand more of working memory, and their complexity and speed of application can reduce available working memory resources.
- Attention to broad design and the degree of autonomy a digital tool allows can contribute to student success.

Sum it up

Working memory is one of the most significant considerations in the classroom for teachers. Digital tools should support the attainment of knowledge, and poorly designed resources can be a notable imposition.

Put it into action

Read more around this subject for additional context. You'll find the work of Ollie Lovell and Peps Mccrea both accessible and immediately relatable to your practice.

Experiment with one part of your practice and attempt to exclude as much extraneous load as possible, and to refine the balance of intrinsic elements.

Appraise your approach with students, being explicit about how and why you are making these changes. When they more clearly understand your motivations, they are more likely to consider what else provides distraction or engagement.

CHAPTER 5

Create and discover

"You can discover more about a person in an hour of play than a year of conversation" – Plato

Sometimes we are forced to work with digital tools that have complexity beyond what we might consider ideal. There's evidence to show that presenting students with instructional 'how to' material in advance of their access to a tool can be of some benefit in improving familiarity and their use of these resources.

This approach does not, however, in my experience, always provide the conditions for all students to be successful in their preparation for, or use of, that tool. Some will read explicit instructions; some will rely on their tacit knowledge to figure it out on the day or lean over to observe the next student and their efforts. Invariably, you can end up wasting time building an understanding about how to best access and employ the tool you're using for the job at hand.

It's important that we also account for the challenges in knowledge transfer when learning a new digital tool in the classroom. A good deal of familiarity and use of the software around us is often gained through trial and error, and often encountered independently. We regularly muddle through on our own when learning how to use a new piece of software, a new app on our phone or resource online.

With a new classroom tool, this approach can be further complicated when we make assumptions about student capacity to use a digital resource. Many young people simply are not as tech savvy as we might give them credit for. They might have strong skills or knowledge in a small range of digital tools they use routinely, but that doesn't mean they will necessarily be capable of picking up a new digital tool and gaining mastery any more briskly. The knowledge they have around the use of a particular clutch of digital tools will not always be transferrable or at all useful in their transition to a new resource.

We use previous experience when encountering a new challenge, such as taking advantage of a new piece of software. We draw on our knowledge base of previous experiences and employ those approaches to find a path through. We often draw on tacit knowledge of software in order to do this, things we've picked up from experience that work but that we may not always be able to articulate as part of our process.

We might intuitively look for navigation features across the top of the screen first, for example, having experienced many times in the past that this is where we might reliably identify the right resources. In doing this, we draw on our knowledge base of what works – or has worked – for us in the past.

We might also look for tutorial tools or a help feature if that's worked reliably for us previously. With well-designed software products, these are likely to lie reliably in a location that's familiar or intuitive. The home button will likely appear in the top left, for example, and the help button might be located somewhere near the top right.

We might also assume certain functions will be available to us if we seek them out, informed by our knowledge base developed in countless other comparable experiences: saving our work, for example, or perhaps knowing an exit button is likely to be available to use if we wish to close the application. When there are fewer options instead of a dizzying display of features, this process of elimination is brisker. We may still be left, however, with the certainty that we might not reach for the most creative approach when using a new digital tool until we have had more experience.

The process of accessing new software can inevitably involve trial and error influenced by a range of experiences that we've had in a myriad of forms both at school and in our own personal use of digital tools.

This process of discovery, of seeking out the purpose of new features and then being bold enough to use them confidently and creatively, perhaps beyond the bounds of what was originally intended for, can also be confronting for some students.

It can also waste a great deal of time in your classroom.

Creative discovery

Creative Discovery is the name I've given to an approach I take to familiarise students with a new digital resource. As the name suggests, it employs a creative approach, one that encourages what might be described as 'left-field thinking' to build familiarity with a new tool, and to better understand the breadth of what's possible with it.

Creative approaches are not innate – they have to be introduced and explained, cultivated like any other new skill. There is no evidence, no body of knowledge that shows us that critical and creative skill development is enhanced by directing students to discover information independently (Sweller, 2022). Students need to be guided in this process. They need exposure to appropriate skills and knowledge that might be employed in order to understand the options available to them.

Most processes that relate to structured creativity can be drawn down to a few key considerations. The first is the development of possibilities and the second is the evaluation of those possibilities (Beghetto, 2020).

If we explore these two areas more closely in the context of forming a creative approach to learning more about digital tools, they might look like the following:

1. Identify the software being evaluated
2. Assess the software features at hand
3. Identify a problem to be resolved within that digital tool
4. Pair the features to aspects of that problem
5. Test the possible features
6. Share the outcome
7. Discuss the cost or benefit

How this should be executed is perhaps served with an example.

I want my students to uncover the features of a new digital tool that will offer them the best opportunity for the expression of their ideas in a way that makes most sense to them. I want them to make strong relational connections between the features available and their ideas on the topic we'll next be exploring.

I also want them to recognise the creative constraints presented by the tool, in order that they are better able to use them to their advantage and possibly stretch the use of the features within the tool – perhaps beyond what was intended by the developer.

Generation

1. I'd suggest after directing students to the tool that they spend a short period identifying the range of features that might allow us to display information or a narrative. You might open a discussion about which features are likely to be most impactful in the use of the tool.

2. Next, identify a subversive use for the tool, something for which it was not intended. You might ask the students how they might approach creating a piece of art with the resource. You might also suggest they consider how they might tell a story with the tool.

For example, if your digital resource is a mind-mapping tool, you might ask how students might use it to tell a story; or if your resource is a chat room, you might ask how it might be used to create a work of art.

Students should be given the freedom to deviate, to approach a problem to be solved in a way that suits them. Identifying a problem to solve lies at the heart, many would argue, of numerous creative endeavours and thinking. So, if a class member wants to work out how to create a rainbow flag with your chat room instead, fantastic. If another wishes to draw a volcano in the mind-mapping tool, that's an equally appropriate approach to take.

Evaluation

1. Tell the story, create the artwork, build the volcano.
2. Now, show and tell. Discuss the features available outlined in your earlier evaluation. How were they employed to best advantage? Colour, for example, might have been used to indicate emotion in a mind-mapped story. Share the student efforts in this space and discuss how they subverted from their possible intended use.
3. You might also reflect with students on those features they didn't have a chance to incorporate into their story or artwork. Allow them the chance to consider alternative views and different ways they might have taken advantage of the resources at hand.

The results of this practice with a class are always visually surprising and varied. When tasked with story writing using a mind-mapping tool, for example, students in my own past classes have produced spiral-pattern stories, long, linear story designs where specific colours dominate and designs that influence meaning.

Often, my experience is that students will take advantage of the feature pallet in the digital tool in ways that indicate new understandings about how the tool can be leveraged in a myriad of unanticipated ways.

After the stories or artworks have been created and shared, students are, in my experience, enthusiastic about the methods they have employed to influence meaning. They are more readily able to see the best applications of this tool to express themselves on any topic, to use the features available to best effect.

One of the additional benefits of this process of discovery is that students will be encouraged to look beyond the bounds of what the developers of other resources may have intended, to think laterally about uses for any resource online.

In short, when students use creative discovery to explore a digital resource, they are encouraged to push the boundaries of what that tool can do to achieve their creative vision.

You might also like to consider using a thinking routine such as See-Think-Make-Discuss to structure your approach. Creative Discovery also shares familiar ground with the Project Zero routine Creative Hunt, which endeavours to encourage us to examine the "limitations of things, and how they might be improved" (Ritchhart, Church & Morrison, 2011). Creative Hunt is also a good routine to encourage students to awaken their creativity to things around them that they had perhaps previously taken for granted.

Setting a time limit is also valuable I've found, and not just because you may want to avoid Creative Discovery taking up an entire lesson. Creative output with limitations demands more critical thought as we consider what can be achieved, how the time might be best served and where to direct the most attention – all key skills to be encouraged. You might think of it in the same way as you would in your approach to writing a sonnet where the limitations in crafting the language are a significant part of the challenge and the appeal.

Creative constraints can inspire us to think laterally about a problem. Some researchers suggest that immediately after working on an activity that involves creative constraints, we are more likely to approach new problems with a greater degree of creativity and objectivity. Sharing creative efforts in this process is key to the longer success of this approach. Students will, in my experience, express glee in subverting the intention of the tools at hand to achieve their own ends. You might also find that returning and including another iterative approach to the creative works is worthwhile.

After your broad discussion, give the students a chance to jump back in and refine their work with their now broader understanding of what other students had achieved. Many creative models include recursion (Runco & Kim, 2018), and recognise that the path to creativity can be messy and not at all linear, and can require a more dynamic and iterative approach, cycling back and forth.

Creative Discovery also helps us empower young adults to set the agenda, rather than letting the resource they are using set it for them. Students using this method are encouraged to consider the way in which digital tools are often designed to shape our output in very specific ways.

When you post on social media, for example, you are bound by the developers' intentions and rules, by their constraints – character lengths that constrict how you express yourself or constraints on the length of video you are allowed to post. These limitations offer creative challenge, but also bind us to the vision of the developer. Encouraging students to think about how they should be served technology, how they might best employ a tool to meet their needs, helps them move beyond these constraints.

It is my strong encouragement in this book that you continue to pursue an ongoing dialogue with your students about the technology they use, how it's best employed and for what purpose. You might also consider a reflective stage to the approach outlined above, allowing students to reflect on when the creative method is needful, and whether a critical evaluation of a tool may be appropriate or useful.

You may employ the process of Creative Discovery in your first use of Excel, for example, but might then follow with a more critical evaluation of the features most appropriate to the task. I would argue, however, that introducing a creative opportunity often allows students to see beyond the bounds of the tool. It also allows students to encounter uncertainty, and to take a structured approach in responding to it.

We often need to draw on creative thinking to find our way around uncertainty, and in some settings uncertainty is provoked – the blank canvas for the art student, for example. Introducing a little uncertainty followed by reflection can allow us to reach beyond our habits and established routines to find new and unique ways to encounter the challenges before us.

ACTIVITY 1

Now that you have both a stronger appreciation for the impact of cognitive load, and an approach designed to build stronger familiarity through a lateral creative approach, it's time to explore your understanding of the two.

Plan a lesson that prepares your students for their use of an intended digital resource and employs the Creative Discovery method.

1. Following the approach outlined above or a variation of it, what tangible evidence do you have of an increased breadth of confidence and knowledge of the digital tool?
2. Where that tool is then employed, what evidence can you find of the breadth of creative use in the sequence of learning that follows?

Key takeaways

- When you need to introduce a new piece of technology with your students, supporting them to think laterally about how it might serve their needs can benefit future applications.

- Seek out creative goals that demand students think beyond or even subvert the intended purpose of a digital tool. Encourage students to explore features in a way that emboldens their use in future problem-solving and, perhaps, other creative pursuits.

Sum it up

Introducing a new digital tool in the classroom should be a considered and reflective process, and by setting a creative goal, students can benefit from a lateral consideration of the use of that tool.

Put it into action

Seek out a new digital tool that meets the design requirements outlined in the earlier chapter; introduce it to students using the Creative Discovery approach.

Discuss with students the way in which the tools they use for work and play can define the work they create with them.

Ask students for an example of a tool they employ routinely outside school, and have them report back in the next lesson on the ways in which its design affects their use.

CHAPTER 6

Routines and features

In this chapter, we'll explore further the five interactions discussed earlier that you'll commonly see in routines. We'll look at each in turn and explain what they are and then explore some approaches you might take when transitioning to them.

The prompts for each transition are explored further in the next chapter. By articulating why we are employing digital tools in our classrooms as we move through sequences of learning, we provide the underpinning of what can become a broader metacognitive understanding.

Discussion tools

Bringing discussion online changes classroom conversation, providing students with a host of new opportunities, whether it's synchronous (live discussion in a video chat, for example) or asynchronous (a discussion over time in spaces such as a discussion forum). Critically, discussion in its various forms is particularly impactful in determining positive outcomes in online learning.

This is because – and it will come as no surprise to any teacher – student relationships and the teacher's voice are significant determinants of success (Gregori, Zhang, Galván-Fernández & De Asís Fernández-Navarro, 2018).

Strong relationships help to support the attainment of strong outcomes, and interaction is essential to successful student learning online or offline (Simonson, Schlosser & Orellana, 2011). Ensuring everyone in the classroom is involved and has a meaningful part to play in any discussion, however, can be challenging.

In an online discussion space, just like the physical classroom space, you can find that it's often the same 25% of students that respond to questions. Sometimes a lack of student response from a portion of your class is due to disengagement, sometimes it can be related to anxiety or perceived social pressure and sometimes it's simply that students aren't called on directly or feel their contributions are not valued sufficiently. There are also other contributing factors – a slow typing speed, for example, that might impact a student significantly in a synchronous chat.

However, an online discussion can offer some surprises, and you may find that the 25% regularly contributing to online discussions include different voices to the 25% contributing to an in-person discussion. Students that are confident and assertive in the classroom may become quiet as mice in an online setting. Others – those that you may not have heard from in the classroom for months – are suddenly emboldened and participate a great deal.

Those five students that always have their hands up are sometimes joined or replaced by those you rarely hear from. For some students, an online discussion offers an opportunity to have a layer of protection around their involvement in an exchange of ideas that wasn't perceived as being present before.

Perhaps one of the principal advantages to online asynchronous discussion is that students are constantly given models from their peers of how to contribute that are more easily replicated. Students can literally cut and paste responses or even pre-prepare some they can paste into the chat space. The record of discussion provides students with an ongoing reference point as they frame their own contributions.

What is key in both synchronous and asynchronous discussion spaces is articulating exactly what it is you want discussed, the roles of those participating and modelling responses as early as possible. Determining the direction you'd like the discussion to head towards is also an important consideration.

The structure of the discussion is another key consideration. Do you want students to respond to each other in a branching exchange, or a question/answer approach? What constraints will you put in place to direct an online chat? If you don't frame it carefully, you'll find very quickly that your online discussion degenerates into wandering discourse or worse – tumbleweeds. Give students a direct purpose in the discussion. Is this a chat about problem-solving? Are you replicating a debate? Are students working towards collective understanding or revealing prior knowledge? Vague direction and open-ended questions will often result in an exchange without purpose or of little value at all.

Teachers ask between 200 and 300 questions in their classrooms to guide discussion each day on average (Brualdi, 1998). That number of questions is often reduced in an online chat, and if the discussion is not clear in its purpose, you'll find it quickly wanders. For this reason, it's also important that you are prepared to interject during the discussion to keep students focused and on task if needed. In my experience, having a few quick phrases prepared that you can cut and paste into the chat to keep things moving is worth the trouble.

Make sure you know what you want to achieve and where you want the discussion to lead your students from the outset to ensure your questions or prompts to foster conversations in the chat are purposeful.

Prompts that link a transition to a discussion space might include:

- "We'll now explore this topic in more depth in a chat room. This will allow us to keep a record of the discussion to review it later, and help to ensure that everyone's voice is heard."

- ○ "We'll explore this idea in a forum that will be open for the rest of the week. Use this space to record your reflections, and to consider other ideas put forward by the class. We'll use our forum because it will allow us to return to our ideas on Friday and examine what we now know about X."

Because of the notably prominent role that synchronous and asynchronous discussion tools play in a blended classroom, we'll look at this particular interaction in more depth on page 93.

Mapping tools

Visual mapping or mind mapping was first developed by Tony Buzan in the 1970s and is an effective strategy to refine thinking, and to visually organise ideas and concepts. Mapping ideas works because we are constantly forced to consider the structure and value of our ideas. It's a metacognitively charged process in which students repeatedly consider how and where to place their ideas, reflections and concepts, and make connections between them.

By visually representing thinking patterns, students not only learn how to accommodate and work with knowledge, but they better understand how new knowledge is created – it also helps them identify and address gaps in knowledge. Connections between ideas are not only more readily recognised, but they are often more easily conveyed and consolidated.

Unproductive study and reflection are a significant impediment to student progress. The beauty of mapping with students is that they see the detail and the steps involved *and* they understand the scope of their efforts. Students are encouraged through visual mapping to better consider hierarchies of knowledge.

Mapping ideas allows students to learn from their peers. They can more readily 'see' the thinking of their classmates, and make connections that they would otherwise have been challenged to reach. Everyone can be an effective learner, and mapping ideas is a strategy that allows teachers to more easily differentiate and to democratise access to knowledge in their classrooms.

Mapping can enable students to move outside the linear path of the learning sequence and stray into more free-form thinking approaches. In a learning sequence, it's where you are best able to make connections and arrive at new understandings based on a spread of sometimes diverse ideas. It's those connections, supported by visual cues, that make mapping a powerful resource, and can lead you towards embedding new understandings.

Prompts that link a transition to a mapping space might include:

- "Now that we've had a chance to discuss what we know about X, let's explore the links between these ideas using our mapping tool. We'll take the key ideas we've identified in our chat room and use the mapping tool to help us explore relationships between these ideas."
- "Consider the three most important ideas you've developed with your partner, now place them in a mind map together."
- "Can I have some suggestions from the class of what the number one influence might be from each team? Let's discuss how to place them on a class mind map together. The map will help us better understand what is common among those ideas."

Sequencing tools

One of my favourite activities in a classroom is the sequencing of ideas, ranking content for prominence or influence, clustering ideas by theme or design, or allowing an exploration of temporal or spatial relationships. Sequencing features in a number of common classroom routines and is often a critical path to understanding when comparing ideas or characteristics. Sequencing can also form an integral part of work in comparative studies.

Tasks that encourage the comparing and contrasting of different elements, or tasks that allow students to clarify relationships, encourage the analysis and recognition of connections between ideas. There is a strong creative element to forging connections, a need to generate new ideas by recognising links between others or from groups of ideas.

It is through the analysis of ideas, say, from a list of sequenced observations, that we are able to evaluate and create new connections. Sequencing allows us to organise data, and better enables us to consider our options when responding to a question.

Students drawing ideas into a sequence are encouraged to see things from a different perspective and to encounter "frequent and repeated patterns" (Muckerheide, Mogill & Mogill, 1999). Sequencing ideas can also be one of the more powerful tools at a teacher's disposal when working with prior knowledge or new knowledge.

Let us return for a moment to our earlier Think-Pair-Share activity. When we visited this routine first, we replaced the 'pair' part of the routine with a chat room. The end result of that online chat is inevitably a transcript of the discussion. Following on from that in the 'share' part of that routine, you might replace a whole-class discussion with a sequencing activity. Sequencing the ideas from the chat is a powerful way to encourage students to reflect on their contributions and to consider information in a new light.

There are dozens of ways you might represent a sequence of ideas. A range of tools might be considered that could include mind-mapping tools, simple tables in Microsoft Word or a linear sequence built in Google Slides.

The key is to consider how much variation you want to allow. What are the creative constraints you want to put in place? How the sequence of learning is framed is as important as the content you are placing within it. There are some wonderful thinking routines to explore that support sequencing. Some like First-Next-Then-Last, for example, guide students to sequence and narrate experience.

Prompts that link a transition to a sequencing space might include:

- ○ "We're now going to rank the prompts we've gathered together in our discussion forum from most influential to least influential. We'll use a sequencing tool to allow us to build our list, and it will help us to understand the importance of each contribution as we add more items."

○ "You've had a chance to explore what you know about X, I'd now like you to use our sequencing tool to list the events in a timeline, which will help us to better understand the order and importance of those events."

Connection tools

Connection features commonly in many classroom routines that stimulate curiosity and inquiry. Connection is often a progressive stage of a routine, where new knowledge is drawn against existing or other new knowledge to encourage new understandings.

Connection can be a critical consideration in relation to our approaches to resolving a problem. Sweller suggests that one method to reduce cognitive load is to approach an issue as 'part whole', that is, that we compartmentalise a problem, breaking it down into individual parts to resolve them one at a time. Sometimes, however, that's simply not possible or practical, and we must look at the problem as a whole first, placing greater demands on our working memory.

To alleviate this, we can use a connected space to provide the scaffolding as we work. We can record persistent examples that are present alongside us in a connection tool as we work, for example. We can use the connected space to collect contributions from student peers and to record their considerations at each stage of a large problem.

By taking these approaches with a digital tool where the purpose is to provide an opportunity for connection, we reduce the ongoing burden on student memory, offloading some of it onto the digital tool.

Connection tools are also often used to support students that have not yet developed the appropriate long-term memories needed to resolve a problem. The notable example here might be times tables. Many students retain them at some point in long-term memory. However, for some, a reference guide is a way to alleviate working memory where the established long-term memory schemas are not yet developed.

In many pedagogical models, connection is represented as a development stage, where we work with new knowledge and reforge it to help us determine new connections, new ways of thinking. Connections can be supported with the use of digital tools that allow us to forge associations such as a polling tool.

Using a template or a worksheet to reflect independently can be one way of encouraging students to make connections, but we are less likely to forge new thinking in a vacuum. We often need collaboration to find success in the connection of new ideas, and student results are stronger when we have collaborative environments online (Cherney, Fetherston & Johnsen, 2018).

Student interaction is not just a preference, it's essential to success (Simonson, Schlosser & Orellana, 2011). Care must be taken, however, that these opportunities are meaningful and purposeful, and when it is part of a thinking routine, this is perhaps more likely to be the case. Fostering these opportunities for students also has strong demonstrated effects on student learning in multiple research studies (Johnson, Johnson & Stanne, 2000).

It is tools that allow us to share, wonder together and inspire each other that often allow us to do this, without which we work at a notable disadvantage in uncovering new thinking.

Prompts that link a transition to a connection space might include:

- "Next, we're going to bring together what we've recorded in our class blog from the last two sessions and connect them in Google Slides. The Slides will help us to structure our ideas, work out how they are related and identify what's missing."

- "In the next activity, we're going to explore some images related to different themes in the novel and place quotes that relate to those themes alongside them. We'll use a table in Google Docs, which will help us to share the examples and examine the different ways these themes are connected in the text."

Reflection tools

Reflection is driven by the way in which we have put our ideas into practice. After we have worked with knowledge and gained new experience from that work, reflection is another way we reach new understandings.

Reflection is often metacognitive in nature, where our new understanding couples with an appreciation of *how* we have learnt as well as *what* we have learnt. A key feature of reflection is the critical thinking involved in tracking the transformation of previous assumptions and beliefs into new knowledge and an expanded self-concept or world view.

Self-regulation is a key feature of reflection. Without rigour in our reflection, without an awareness of the purpose of the reflective task, we are unlikely to uncover and retain new understandings. One of the most powerful forms of reflection follows the use of worked examples, where students reflect on a process and articulate the approach they will need to take in attempting to replicate a successful effort outlined by the teacher.

Reflection is often also a more personal phase in a learning sequence. Allowing students to identify the way they can most readily make meaning from their experiences is a significant aspect in their growth as a learner. Reflection can be achieved through written response, but also through audio, video narration, drawing and a host of other modalities. Don't constrain your students to one path – encourage them to experiment with different modes. As Rogers (2001) observes, "Perhaps no other concept offers... as much potential for engendering lasting and effective change in the lives of students as that of reflection."

Prompts that link a transition to a reflection space might include:

- "In this next task, we're going to record audio files about the way in which we can use the approaches we've seen successfully applied in this problem. We'll use these audio files as a reference we can refer back to and to support our work as we move through this unit."

- "I'd now like you to jump into your blog and reflect on what you now know about X. These reflections will allow us to look back later to better understand how our ideas may have changed."

Key takeaways

- Identifying interactions in a sequence of learning that are common to classroom routines can help us to better align digital tools within that sequence.

- Discussion, mapping, sequencing, connection and reflection are five interactions common to core classroom routines. Recognising the value of each type of interaction and in order to articulate the value of that interaction is key to developing strong transition statements.

Sum it up

By aligning digital tools under five interactions that appear in common routines, we can begin to recognise how and where they best align in support of those routines. Articulating why we are using that digital tool with that type of interaction supports a stronger understanding of the purpose and value of that tool.

Put it into action

Look back on your contributions in the earlier activities where you defined the types of tools you commonly use and the classroom routines you set them against. Are there any interactions where alternate simple tools might replace those you had nominated?

Switch one simple digital tool with another in those earlier tables. How does this change or redefine the routine?

CHAPTER 7

Transitions

By employing Simple Tools in our classroom, we increase our capacity to build meta-knowledge, a critical consideration when we work with technology. The reasons we employ the digital tools we use should not be a secret to our students and their purpose should not be clouded or a surprise.

We should be explicit and reflective with our students about the digital tools we use. Outlining the rationale for our transition not only increases buy-in from our students, but they develop an increasing appreciation for the reason they are undertaking a sequence of learning.

In the previous chapter, we looked at some examples of transition prompts as we move between digital tools. In this chapter, we'll look a little more closely at those statements to better understand the purpose and benefit of making these links explicit.

The more we work to clarify and demystify the purpose for employing specific digital tools, the greater efficacy and agency our students will gain on their learning journey. We also need to be clear in our own teaching and learning about the reasons we are employing specific digital tools. We must be able, as teachers, to articulate why a specific digital tool is best aligned with specific content, and the pedagogical approach that is best employed for that content and that digital tool.

Transitions between digital tools are important and should be purposeful and considered as we shift between each phase of a sequence of learning. It's critical that we are explaining the purpose of each transition, in order that students understand how and why they are shifting to a new digital tool, and how it relates to the new stage of their learning sequence. There's evidence that metacognitive reflection is a teachable skill that is central to other domain general skill sets, such as problem-solving and critical thinking.

We need to support our young people to develop a metacognitive awareness of why they are using the digital tools they employ. We need to help them to become independent learners, confident about the best way to employ the digital resources at their disposal.

There has never been so much informal learning made possible through technology, and with that breadth of access and the continual significant growth of options at our fingertips, these skills have never been more important.

When you begin teaching students about the value of the digital tools they are using and reflecting with them on that value in transitions in your learning sequence, they will benefit from your being explicit about the how and why. Students don't yet have the schema in place, the mental muscle memory that allows them to understand reflexively in what way the digital tool could be useful. We need to give students the appropriate scaffolding that allows them to self-explain the purpose and benefit of the digital tools we use with them.

Transition in a learning sequence

> *"If we don't understand something, we can't control it. If we don't control it, we can't improve it"* – Dr H James Harrington

There are many studies that show that even simple fill-in-the-blank scaffolding can lead to much stronger learning outcomes during the early adoption of an idea. As you move about the classroom, providing guidance on the next part of your learning sequence, the reasons for a transition to a new digital tool should be easily understood and explicit.

We want at each transition point to be clear about where we've come from, where we are going and where it might lead us:

"We are moving from our chat room where we were able to reveal what we already knew about storms to our mind-mapping tool. That's going to help us better understand how those ideas are connected. What we might find, is that by doing that, we'll come to a new understanding about storms."

We must provide students with the tools that will allow them, when they are confronted by a similar challenge, to interrogate which digital tool will be most appropriately leveraged to solve the problem in front of them. At an early developmental stage, providing students with the sentence stems they can use to understand the value of those tools is a solid strategy.

Prompts help lead students towards being able to self-explain the purpose of those tools as they work with them. Students being able to apply those same explanations independently in new circumstances is our goal. The more organised and established their understanding of the purpose and function of digital tools is, the greater our capacity for strategic application later.

We need to support students to build these long-term memories of the purpose and function of the digital tools they employ. The more comprehensive and organised these memories are for students, the better they will be able to employ those schemas in their studies and beyond. We want their understanding of the purpose of their use to become familiar, as it is through that familiarity that we gain proficiency, which often leads to deeper conceptual understanding.

Mccrea (2017) tells us that early long-term memories are, "Blurry, only partially formed and not clearly distinct from similar concepts. Simple, basic in structure, with superficial connections to related concepts. Shallow, tied tightly to particular contexts and not easily applied to different situations."

When we use prompts to guide student thinking and understanding of the how and why of a transition in a learning sequence, each time they gain a more cemented understanding of the possible future applications of the tools they are working with.

There are three types of prompts that are seen in the literature as commonly effective:

> **Process prompts:** helping students to better understand their own thinking of a process or procedure.
>
> **Connection prompts:** supporting them to unpack the connections between ideas. 'How does this connect with' or 'what is similar about'. These are also prompts that relate to the sequence of learning, and how the next digital tool, the next step, relates to the previous or following stage in the learning sequence.
>
> Connection prompts can also relate to the different combinations of tool use, explaining how use of one tool corresponds and supports the use of the next; for example, unpacking the transcript of a chat discussion on a tool that supports sequencing or ranking.
>
> **Anticipation prompts:** guiding students towards what might happen next, and in doing so, appreciating the purpose of their next task more readily.

In each of the examples that follow, you'll see examples of these prompts for you to consider as you determine your own prompts aligned with the digital tools you've settled upon in your learning sequence.

Once your students have understood the way in which a chat room discussion can be folded into a mapping exercise, for example, and why they are using each tool to benefit their understanding, they will increasingly appreciate the value of each tool in that sequence of learning and its broader application.

Reflection for students

Moreno and Mayer (2007) tell us that students need time to reflect during learning, in order to allow them the best opportunity to integrate and organise new information. Transition statements are one way of providing students with the opportunity to reflect upon the value of the work just concluded, on how it relates to the next task and where it might lead them.

While initially the transition statements are likely to be heavily teacher-led, the goal is for students to enact them of their own volition. Our goal is empowered learners who understand the value of each new digital tool, its purpose in a learning sequence and how to employ it to solve their own future challenges.

Teaching with digital tools is different and does constitute a shift in practice, but that doesn't mean you have to leave your previous pedagogy behind. For most teachers, the shift to learning online is notable, but often not as significant a change in practice as they imagine. Much of what they already know can be translated to an online space.

Exit tickets are one way that teachers commonly ask students to reflect on their achievement and learning that has taken place. For example, employ a simple survey at the end of a lesson:

> **Red:** Today, I was frustrated because...
>
> **Yellow:** Today, I considered a new approach or a new perspective...
>
> **Green:** Today, I learnt and understood...

This approach is a sound way of introducing reflection, however, consider the yellow question in particular. In this mid-stage, students are reflecting on *how* they learnt, rather than *what* they learnt.

The evidence tells us that students that reflect on the method of their learning are more likely to perform more strongly than those that do not (Mason, Boldrin & Ariasi, 2010; Dignath & Büttner, 2008).

Darling-Hammond, Austin, Cheung and Martin, in their (2003) work, explain that there are two types of metacognition: reflection and self-regulation. The first is about understanding what we know, while the second is about how we approach learning.

Self-regulation is bound up in our capacity to modify our approach, and being aware of when that might be needed. To do this effectively, we need to have not only a clear sense of the goal ahead, but we should be aware of when we might be drifting off-course and need to self-correct.

Attentional awareness is therefore a skill we must be cognisant of in our support of students as they develop increased independence in their learning.

Metacognitive strategies in the classroom should support students to better understand what they already know and help them to articulate what they may have learnt and how that was achieved. The purpose is also to help them set their own goals by supporting reflection on their progress, evaluating their efforts and helping them to identify more effective strategies when striving towards a goal.

The use of simple digital tools supports this process by making the purpose and benefit of employing a particular digital resource more apparent, allowing the student to better discern its value in the learning process and to understand how to transfer its use from one context to another.

Also of note in Darling-Hammond et al's 2003 work is the suggestion that in order for effective metacognition to take place, students should be at the centre of the discussion, allowing them to do most of the talking, and that this should take place before, during and after the learning experience.

We want students engaged in acts of intrinsic feedback, that is, personal reflection as a consequence of an action taken as it relates to their intended goal. We should encourage reflection on the value of the method they employed to reach that conclusion and the tool used to get there. As students consider the outcome of their efforts and compare the result to what they had intended or assumed would be the outcome, the choice of digital tool should feature stridently.

Was it the right digital tool for the job? Should they have considered another approach with a different tool that may have led to a more successful outcome? What other digital tools and learning approaches might have created alternate opportunities and outcomes? Simple tools with a clear purpose and an articulated place in learning make this reflection more practical and achievable.

The domain general skills that relate to problem-solving and creation, those that impact upon all subject areas formally and informally, should be deeply informed by a sound knowledge of how and why we employ the digital tools we use.

In order for students to reach this point, to understand and appreciate the value and purpose of the digital tools they employ to solve problems and reach conclusions, we must provide the metacognitive steps that allow them this reflection. We also need to give students the opportunity to reflect and understand, to articulate and self-explain.

For example, you may be using a chat room to guide students in a developmental stage of a sequence of learning. You intend the chat room to provide the opportunity for shared reflection about pollution in the local creek. You also know that you hope to use the transcript in the next activity to allow you to rank the ideas generated across the class, and to create an opportunity for shared understandings and to broaden knowledge.

Let's look at the practical reality of reflecting on our approach in the classroom in an example.

> **First, we should explain our plan, the what:**
>
> We're now going to use tlk.io to chat about what we know about pollution in the creek.
>
> **Then, we'll reveal the why and how – why we chose this digital tool and how it will support development of the kind we need for this inquiry:**
>
> Can anyone suggest why we're using this tool?
>
> Pause.

Another reason is to give everyone some time to think about their responses and allow you to look at what other people are contributing to the chat room. Sometimes when we see another person's idea, that can help to remind us of something we'd forgotten.

Now, we explain how it will support that next stage of development:

When we finish using the chat room, we'll take a record of the chat and look at all of our ideas in one place. Why do you think that might be helpful?

You might also use this last reflection at a midpoint in the activity, to lift the rigour of the contributions as well as to ensure that students are aware that we will continue to work with the knowledge we are generating.

You may also wish to ask the students to predict the outcome based on their previous use of the tool. Encouraging this type of anticipation will achieve these two things:

1. It allows you to assess how well they appreciate the benefit of using that tool.
2. Prediction is a metacognitive strategy that requires the students to consider the goal and how they will strive towards it.

This is, of course, a simpler consideration when the purpose of the resource and the approach are clear, and when the goal is well understood. It's also important that you provide the opportunity to reflect on the success of that strategy during and/or at the completion of the task.

There are lots of digital tools we might have used in this activity with our class. We might instead have asked students to sequence the ideas they have in a small group in a shared document. Or we might have used a collaborative mind-mapping tool to create a broad map of the class ideas, so an important part of our reflection is necessary to reflect on whether this was the right tool for the job.

Our next questions to the class following the activity could be:

Do you think this was the best digital tool to use in this activity?

What was similar about the work we've done today in the chat room compared with when we reflected using our mind-mapping tool last week? What was different about it?

Do you think the chat room was the right digital tool to use to help us understand all the issues that are present at the creek?

Of course, we also need a point of reference to determine our success:

Who can tell us what the intention of this activity was, and who feels that we were able to achieve that goal with this tool?

For a moment, let's return to the principles of simple digital tools. They are fast to employ in the classroom, allowing us to move with fewer impediments through a sequence of learning. They are also clear in their purpose, making answering this question more straightforward.

What we want students to appreciate is the breadth of digital tool options available to them, and how each one will create different opportunities for reflection and learning.

It's also important that we recognise at this point that there are two ways students will reflect on the importance of the use of these tools. The first is extrinsic, with the teacher guiding the student to reflect on the value of the tool they have employed as we've indicated above. The second – and our ultimate goal – is intrinsic, where the student employs a digital tool and, as a consequence of their use, observes and can articulate its benefit and value in relation to the objective they are striving for.

Reflection is for teachers, too!

For teachers, the decision around which tool to use is also, of course, a central consideration. Why are we electing to choose one digital tool over another? While teachers bring their content knowledge and pedagogical knowledge to bear in the classroom, they must also give serious consideration to how they relate and are impacted by the digital tools they use. Which digital tool is most appropriately paired with which pedagogical approach, and with which content?

This model of reflection is called Technological, Pedagogical and Content Knowledge (TPACK), developed by Mishra and Koehler (2006), and is a powerful model for directing teacher reflection towards the most appropriate digital tool that best meets our pedagogical needs, and that is best suited to the content with which we wish to work.

For the student to understand a metacognitive approach, the thinking behind it must be modelled by the teacher. Students need to see and understand their own metacognitive thinking to support student reflection of the same kind. In other words, teachers must first understand the purpose of their choice of a digital tool and how it relates to the strategy they are employing in the classroom.

When the digital tool we wish to employ is straightforward in its purpose and when it does one thing particularly well, then it is more straightforwardly evident which pedagogical approach and content may be best suited.

The beauty of having a range of simple tools at your disposal is that when one doesn't result in the outcome you were hoping for, you're far more empowered to move to another resource. With simple digital tools at your fingertips, you may have students electing to use an alternate tool to attempt to reach the same goals within the lesson.

With complex digital tools that perform multiple functions with a myriad of resources and features, the purpose of the tool can make this decision more challenging and less clear. With a selection of simple digital tools at your disposal, you can more easily discern how and why they are best paired with a particular pedagogical approach or may be suited to a specific content.

In the same way, our goal for students must be to empower them with the metacognitive clarity that will enable them to reflect upon the digital tools at their disposal and allow them to discern whether it be for collaborative work or content creation, idea generation or reflection, or perhaps to build connections between ideas, to have the clarity of understanding which tool will benefit their inquiry the most.

The more opportunities we give our students to act critically on how and why they are employing one digital tool over another in pursuit of new knowledge, the better equipped they will be to make astute and thoughtful choices in all avenues of lifelong learning – both formal and informal.

We want students to see beyond the surface of the tools they use, to understand and more deeply appreciate the structural advantage the tools they use offer in resolving a problem. Tools that are best designed to guide them towards a specific type of thinking or that provide a platform best designed to resolve a particular type of puzzle.

To provide the right opportunity for students to self-reflect, we need to offer them the opportunity in a learning sequence to pause and consider what's possible. They need to see how we make those choices, rationalise from the range of digital tools available which might be best and evaluate their effectiveness. This type of analogical reasoning allows students to appreciate the principles that underlie the digital tool choices they make, to see the patterns of success they can transfer to new problems they encounter.

Finding that success takes a good deal of practice. Students require multiple opportunities to select and refine their choices, to self-reflect upon which tool might be or was the right choice to make for a particular problem.

Our skill in applying the right strategies for the right problems is gained by solving them – many of them!

Some strategies you might employ with students towards finding the right digital tools are:

- Guessing and checking
- Making a reference list of the tools available, linked with possible outcomes
- Providing a list where a choice is made by eliminating possibilities
- Using a direct reasoning technique
- Considering a simpler problem first that might align better with a specific digital tool
- Writing a statement on the type of tool to select and why, then interrogate it

To help guide students towards these reflections, it can be helpful to have a reference point as you shift from one digital tool to the next in your learning sequence.

Prompt structures

Consider the following prompt structures when you are employing a learning sequence with your students to help you determine how best to frame the reasons you are, as a class, determining one digital tool over another. I've based the examples below on the methods of approach indicated in the work of Entwistle and Peterson (2004), which centres on encouraging students towards outcomes with fewer misconceptions in their studies.

Did this digital tool (discussion, mapping, sequencing, connection, reflection)...

- Guide us towards having a broader view of the problem?
- Help us to connect some of the things we knew already to new ideas?
- Support us in identifying any big ideas that were common among the issues?

- Provide the right space to check the evidence we have?
- Allow us to reach new conclusions about what we knew before?

Was it the right digital space or tool to…

- Support us as we reflected on what we already know?
- Help us to engage with new ideas?
- Help to challenge us and the ideas we already held about this issue?

I'd also suggest that it can be helpful to have in mind at which stage of Bloom's taxonomy you are working in as you guide students towards a metacognitive reflection on their employment of a digital tool. If the work you are undertaking mainly involves basic recall and understanding, such as the development of and practice in recalling a list of character names in a novel, then your reflection might, for example, look something like this:

Was this the right tool to help us…

- Define the facts?
- Reveal the positions of the characters?
- Support us in classifying who was who in the book?
- Guide us to recognise the structure of the novel?

Or perhaps you may be working with students to create their own new original creative works. In that case, your reflections may be something like this:

Was this the right tool to help us…

- Justify our approach as the right one?
- Design our new work?
- Form new conclusions?
- Investigate other possibilities in the work?

Intended outcome

Critical to our reflection is, of course, the evidence of whether the learning intention has been reached. Do the students have a clear sense that they have reached their intended goal? How are they determining what success looks like? It's crucial that going into the activity students also have a clear sense of what the intended outcome is at the other end.

We don't always make the right choice or reach the conclusion we were looking for. Rather than repeat the same mistake, it's particularly valuable to have the opportunity to reflect on our lack of success, hypothesise a new approach and employ a new digital tool and method. Or, it might not be the tools we've employed but the sequence in which we used them – or perhaps our goal has been the wrong one; we've focused on what we know about pollution in the creek but perhaps our goal is too broad or too narrow. Again, understanding the intended outcome is necessary if we are to have a point of reference.

The key is in knowing that working with knowledge can take many forms. We must empower students to reflect on how the digital tool choice we've made is the right fit for our purpose, and direct them towards the development of intrinsic understandings of how to best employ the digital resources at their disposal.

An elephant in the room

Of course, we may have what we consider to be an ideal pedagogical approach and the perfect digital tool at the ready to explore our content, but there is another significant consideration as we determine and then articulate and discuss the digital tools we use: context.

Our students come to the classroom with a broad range of experience, both educationally but also culturally, and with varying degrees of trauma, social or emotional challenges and perhaps medical impositions. Their individual contexts can have an enormous impact on the successful use of the digital tool we employ in any sequence of learning.

Knowing your students and understanding that context can be of critical importance both to the relevance of the digital tool we select and their capacity to use it alongside peers in a way that allows for meaningful involvement in the learning at hand.

The value of simple tools can be notable as we contend with this context. Simple tools selected for their thoughtful and purposeful design often reflect heuristics that accommodate broader accessibility in the classroom. A student with low processing, for example, will be able to contend far more readily with a simple chat space than one that includes a dozen additional features that simply aren't necessary to engage with the task at hand.

The additional benefit for the use of simple tools when contending with context is the capacity of the teacher to swiftly employ an alternate digital tool for that student, to allow them to negotiate with their explicit content in a meaningful way. A student that is, for example, challenged by engagement in an online discussion due to anxiety can be quickly directed to a simple mapping tool to allow them to participate in a different way. Or, perhaps we might direct that student to a shared document they might use to start drawing the class contributions to the chat into a sequence that everyone can use later.

The key to this final part of our reflection is to ensure that student observations on the success of the use of a digital tool must be individual. While a consensus view is valuable, the right tool must be employed to suit each student's individual context and learning needs. Students must be given the opportunity to appreciate that a flexible and independent use of digital tools to reach the same outcome is sometimes needful.

Reflecting on your learning makes demands on your working memory just like anything else you turn your mind to. Checking in with your students to encourage them to reflect on their progress and consideration of the value of their current approach will also disrupt their focus. For these reasons, it's important not to expect too much all at once. Introduce these approaches gradually, and you'll reap the benefits as students gain a stronger appreciation for how and why they are using the digital tools available to them.

Build these approaches into your classroom routines and make them a part of your every day, and not an added extra. By doing this you'll be developing an environment that supports self-reflection and interrogation that for students will simply be a part of their natural workflow rather than an add-on.

Consider this Bloom's table to help you determine language that might be appropriate to the type of activity you're engaged with. These verbs will help you to better create transition statements that help encourage reflection on the purpose and measure of the digital tools you employ. Some verbs work across the Bloom spectrum, and so you'll find some repeated in the table at different levels.

Creating, designing, constructing, planning, producing, inventing, devising, making	Reflecting, building, adapting, collaborating, composing, directing, devising, broadcasting, resource building, writing, recording, programming, simulating, role-playing, solving, remixing, facilitating, designing, negotiating, leading
Evaluating, checking, hypothesising, critiquing, experimenting, judging, testing, detecting, monitoring	Arguing, debating, validating, testing, scoring, assessing, criticising, commenting, iterating, pivoting, defending, detecting, experimenting, grading, hypothesising, judging, moderating, posting, predicting, rating, reflecting, reviewing (for example, a service or platform), editorialising
Analysing, comparing, organising, deconstructing, attributing, outlining, finding, structuring, integrating	Calculating, categorising (for example, web content, search results, etc), breaking down, correlating, deconstructing, strategic hyperlinking, supporting (for example, a cause), mind-mapping, organising, appraising, advertising, dividing, deducing, distinguishing, illustrating, questioning, structuring, integrating, attributing, estimating, explaining

Applying, implementing, carrying out, using, executing	Acting out, articulating, re-enacting, loading, choosing, determining, displaying, revising search keywords, executing, examining, implementing, sketching, experimenting, hacking, interviewing, painting, preparing, playing, integrating, presenting, charting
Understanding, interpreting, summarising, inferring, paraphrasing, classifying, comparing, explaining, exemplifying	Annotating, tweeting, associating, tagging (tagging your curriculum, for example), summarising, relating, categorising, paraphrasing, predicting, comparing, contrasting, commenting, journaling, interpreting, grouping, inferring, estimating, extending, gathering, exemplifying, expressing
Remembering, recognising, listing, describing, identifying, retrieving, naming, locating, finding	Copying, defining, finding, locating, quoting, listening, googling, repeating, retrieving, outlining, highlighting, memorising, networking, searching, identifying, selecting, tabulating, duplicating, matching, curating and bookmarking, bullet-pointing

Key takeaways

- Purposeful transitions clearly articulated are a crucial step in ensuring students are aware of the benefit of each digital resource in their learning. They also benefit teachers, guiding us towards a clear alignment with pedagogy and content.
- Metacognition is a teachable skill and should be aligned with digital tool use.
- Prompts that enhance attentional awareness, that explain process, connection and that provide anticipation and direction are needful.
- Structured transitions are essential, spaces for reflection are crucial.
- An appreciation for the complexities that context brings to these transitions is a notable requirement.

Sum it up

Mindful, structured transitions that support student reflection and clear metacognitive strategies that enhance intrinsic understanding of the right approach and digital tool can enhance student achievement. Appreciating student context and its broad influence can be key to student success.

Put it into action

Take a measured approach and be explicit in your transition between two digital tools, or to a single digital tool in your class.

Ask students to take on a critical role in evaluating the use of that tool in pursuit of its intended purpose.

CHAPTER 8

Collaboration and discussion online

The research tells us clearly that teachers working with digital tools in the classroom – and particularly when teaching remotely – must prioritise the development of skills that foster interaction and communication. Digital tools that allow for collaboration and discussion, both synchronous and asynchronous, deserve, therefore, a special mention in this book, simply because they are so crucial in online teaching in today's world of COVID-19 and remote delivery.

Our selection of the best tools, and our understanding of how they are best employed with specific content and the right pedagogical approach, should be a notable priority. Having a good sense of the range of ways you can best support student collaboration, community development and discussion with digital tools in a sequence of learning is therefore a huge advantage.

In this final chapter, we return to the discussion phase explored in chapter 6 to look at some of the considerations you should have in this important feature of online delivery. This is not an exhaustive list, but a small catalogue of what I've seen work well in synchronous and asynchronous collaborative spaces. It's also a synthesis of some of what we know works well in blended environments.

Code switching and language online

Sometimes when switching between spaces in which students are invited to contribute, we need to adjust our language to best suit the activity and intended learning outcome. Code switching is the process of switching from one dialect or language to another depending on the situation. We all code switch to a greater or lesser degree, adjusting our language to better suit different friendship groups or different online spaces. Different spaces and people can require us to adjust the language we use, and this is often particularly evident in online spaces.

Many young people do this all the time, presenting a different persona with explicit language choices for different spaces online. They might use more colloquial language, for example, when posting on Snapchat, but when using Instagram, they might have a particular look and feel they are pursuing and elect to use language that's more poised and tagged to appeal to a specific audience. A chat over Discord, however, might be more relaxed or profane!

In the classroom, attention to the sort of language you wish to articulate in the online spaces you provide is equally important, because if you don't set the tone, your class will. It needs to be apparent in the examples you seed into discussion spaces and made clear as you transition between different digital tools.

The language you employ has a strong bearing on how an issue will be explored, the degree of reflection that may take place and how relaxed or formally students will respond. New vocabulary is a common cause of high cognitive load for students (Lovell, 2020).

It's particularly important, therefore, to make appropriate space for those students that don't yet have a grasp of the breadth of language specific to the task that's required to appropriately understand and articulate a view. For this reason alone, code switching can be an important consideration as you move through a learning sequence.

If you encourage emoticons and 'casual' language, then the outcome of an activity may be more reflective and exploratory, and sometimes result in a more personal response. Students may need this more casual approach, particularly when broaching a new topic. An opportunity to use their existing vocabulary to explore the topic at hand, to frame it in their own words, can make it notably more accessible.

As students develop a better understanding of a topic and are able to more readily use complex language associated with the content, a transition to more formal language may be appropriate. Explicitly code switching in the classroom and moving to more formal language helps students reframe the discussion and can add a layer of rigour. Not only that, but it will quickly assist you in establishing who in the class still struggles with key concepts.

Transcripts from a discussion in a simple chat space or class forum can also allow you to quickly determine which students are employing an appropriate breadth of vocabulary specific to the topic, and those that are still attempting to grasp it.

Of course, a discussion of what language is appropriate more broadly is crucial. Negotiating discussion protocols before you have a problem and aligning your discussion with your school values, for example, can greatly support a smooth transition to a new activity within a digital tool.

Most students will already have experience chatting online or on the phone with friends and will be able to suggest considerations for what is and what is not appropriate. I find that sometimes a simple method of describing my expectations around formal language is to explain that I am looking for the language they might use in an essay. Of greatest importance, however, is asking for their opinion in defining good behaviour and appropriate language in the online spaces you inhabit with them.

I have always found with my own students that the class will have very defined views about what is and what is not appropriate. Many of them will have experience in negotiating language, sensitive topics and contending with people online that are happy and even eager to take things too far. A good set of online discussion expectations defined with your students will help to establish a space that is safe and productive.

Don't underestimate the power of your own contributions in modelling language appropriate for the space. Your timely interjection can quickly shift the focus and language suitable to the discussion.

Sometimes the difference between casual and more formal responses can also be simply providing the appropriate amount of time to reflect. Placing a time limit on discussions can also be a good way of ensuring contributors retain a focus on the expected outcomes of the activity. A time limit also encourages a sense of expectation and a competitive spirit, and draws students together through a sense of urgency.

Preparatory work

While traditional representations of Think-Pair-Share offer students time for reflection, comparison and sharing, an asynchronous discussion also allows some students time to prepare a more formal response. An online discussion space allows students to look at multiple perspectives that have already been put forward, and to frame their own position while reflecting on that greater breadth of responses. Some students in particular need this time to reflect, to consider alternatives and prepare their position. There are always students that need more time to process information and to consider their views.

Sometimes, however, you simply don't have the luxury of taking things slowly. Students that may be impeded from responding quickly can, in these cases, be at a disadvantage. Asking them to prepare some statements in advance is a key strategy towards ensuring they are able to meaningfully take part in an online discussion.

A simple Word document with pre-prepared position points they can cut and paste into a chat room can not only allow them the opportunity to take a more prominent part in discussions, it also allows them to feel that they are meaningfully contributing.

You might also prepare some sentence stems with some students that they can use to applaud good ideas or to deepen the discussion:

- "I see what you mean, but I wonder if..."
- "I appreciate your contribution because..."
- "Have you also considered...?"

Set a quota

It's worth considering setting a fixed number of contributions students can make in an online space. For example, you might ask a chat room with six students to each contribute a maximum of five ideas. You may request that students only add three of their ideas to an online mind map or that they make only three or four connections from existing ideas in that map.

By setting a limit on the number of ideas students can contribute, you encourage those with a hundred ideas to reflect on the handful most worthy. You also make the task more manageable for students that are reluctant to put forward any suggestions.

It's important that you encourage this limitation in a positive way. "I know you all have a bunch of ideas on this topic, but I'm limiting you to five each! I realise that will be difficult, but I'm confident you'll work out which ideas are most important and choose only the best five for each of you."

By limiting the conditions of their involvement with a creative constraint, students are forced to reflect more deeply on their participation and contribution.

Projecting and intruding

Things do not always go as planned. Sometimes discussions or contributions in shared online spaces get off track. Perhaps you haven't stipulated the subject of discussion clearly enough or outlined the task succinctly and students have gotten off topic. Or perhaps students are exploring the surface of the problem or deliberately straying from the task, exploring subject matter more suitable to the playground.

There are several approaches you might take where this occurs:

- Ask one student to take on a role. This doesn't have to be a supervisory role, it might be that they put on their metaphorical 'black hat' (Edward de Bono, 2022), providing an alternate reflective position. If you're working in a collaborative mind map, you might have one student simply looking for opportunities to connect ideas, or to question the links between them.

- Ask one student in each group to act as an authority on a topic at hand. The role might be that of an author or a scientist perhaps. Try to identify a student for this role that has a sound grasp of the vocabulary specific to the topic at hand.

- Who does the topic impact upon? This is sometimes a good way to provide a role for students. Ask who is impacted by decisions on this topic, and then consider the roles that might be provided to students based on the answer. For example, if the discussion is about a class novel, you might assign some students the role of a character to respond to questions, or that discusses key themes. If the discussion is about pollution in the local river, then perhaps students may take on roles of local residents, council members in the area, business interests, etc.

- While some students are happy to be performative in the classroom, others can be reluctant to take on a position, feeling that it will place them under a spotlight. In an online space, however, that student can more easily take on a role and present themselves as the author or a character in a novel, or perhaps a prominent historical figure. This can be further supported by offering them the opportunity to prepare statements or comments they can cut into the chat space in advance.

Lurkers

This term is often used to describe members of an online community that are reluctant to actively participate or simply choose not to and watch on without taking part instead. This behaviour can often be linked to anxiety, feelings of inadequacy in the online space or a sense that the light shone on them in a discussion area is too bright.

For several years, I would regularly poll my students, surveying them on their contributions in my classroom to get a sense of their varying degrees of comfort and confidence. One of the things that became clear over time is that online spaces are, for some, a way of connecting without being seen. For some, the attraction of being in a chat room online or commenting on a video is that they are anonymous and yet their participation is noted. They can hide behind a persona and feel connected and yet remain remote and protected – at least to a degree. In an online space their participation is often clearly linked to who they are, and that can be confronting when much of your other participation in online spaces has been anonymous.

To counteract this and to encourage greater participation, Harkins and Petty's (1982) work suggests two solutions. The first is to increase the significance of the task, making it more challenging. The second is to encourage individual tasks among participants in order that their involvement is more defined.

A good way to identify a lurker in your online discussions is to review the transcripts and highlight contributions from your suspects. You'll find it becomes quickly apparent who the lurkers are in your classroom.

Once you've identified them, one way to support your lurkers is to help them to prepare several contributions before the chat. Give them the discussion topic in advance and allow them a little more thinking time. Another approach is to partner them with another student with poor typing skills, increasing the likelihood that they will have to take the driver's seat in the discussion. Finally, give your reluctant contributor the opportunity to practice participating in the chat space. Hold a low-level small-group discussion on a topic they are comfortable with.

Because discussion can move quickly in a chat room, and because some students can type faster than others, a large group can be difficult to manage. Not to mention the fact that in a large group online, individual participants can feel their contributions are quickly lost in the crowd. Conversations can become convoluted with too many competing voices. For this reason, groups of no more than six are often best in a synchronous chat room online.

Isolation

Online spaces can be isolating and impersonal. It can take time to build trust – even when your students have also had the experience of spending time in the classroom together. Small consistent groups are often a good way to quickly encourage that trust.

- Ensuring students contribute on similar schedules can also be an advantage. While asynchronous discussion can occur over time, students relish the opportunity to see their contribution responded to quickly.

- Nominating a leader can also help, selecting a person in each small group you are confident will drive discussion forward. You might consider ensuring that, before students contribute, they have a chance to consider how they will respond together. A synchronous chat prior to contributing to a forum can help students rehearse their ideas and determine a way forward.

- Sometimes broaching a topic together in a discussion space can be a great way to encourage responses later. For example, making contributions to a class form together in a live class and talking about the value of each response can be the spur to continue that discussion later after the class. This approach is particularly good when introducing a new discussion space, and allows you to set the tone and expectation clearly.

- Carefully directing peer reflection can be a powerful way of encouraging all students to contribute thoughtfully. Take care, however, if you elect to do this, to ensure that students have had an opportunity to practice responding to each other in advance. Tone can often be misunderstood in asynchronous spaces. I'm sure we have all had the experience of receiving an email where the tone could not be easily determined.

- Finally, take the long view. In my experience, setting a clear expectation for when you want full participation from all students and planning for it also ensures that your own goal is more manageable and achievable. Ensure that planning for student contributions takes account of reluctance, isolation and possible anxiety, and plan to ease them into it.

One concern that I've often seen, for example, is teachers exasperated by students not turning on webcams in synchronous spaces when logging in from home. Rather than becoming frustrated, consider a staged approach to their visual involvement. Ask them to turn on cameras but place a toy in front of the camera if they are anxious, for example.

Another good trick is to encourage students in a game at the start of the lesson that requires webcam use. A scavenger hunt is a good way of kicking off the lesson with a fun activity that has low stakes and involves a camera. Ask students to find simple objects and race back to the online classroom within an allotted time.

Give your students time to make the transition to full involvement and provide them with clear strategies to achieve that. You'd never expect a student to encounter new content in your subject without scaffolding the appropriate skills and knowledge to approach it. The same is true for their involvement online. Just because they are using social media in a variety of ways does not mean they will be comfortable or have the necessary skills to participate in discussions in an online classroom in the same way.

Moderation

What form of moderation you can employ in an online discussion chat space is an important consideration.

Some online spaces will allow a full set of discussion-monitoring tools, inappropriate-language filters and user-access tools. In my experience, however, with careful implementation in the classroom, these simply aren't necessary.

More features can mean more distraction – for you and your class. Students quickly become aware of the blocking methods and either find ways around them or choose not to actively take part. Worst of all, when you moderate a discussion online with too much vigour, you can be seen to be heavy-handed, and students are less likely to enjoy the experience. It may even devalue the learning space.

A careful interjection during the discussion can be a powerful way of ensuring appropriate language and behaviour are on the agenda. A quick interruption in the chat space to encourage them at the beginning and a short interjection during the discussion, "You guys are doing really well, keep up the good work!" or "You seem to have wandered off the topic a little, why don't we return to the discussion sentence posted earlier?" You may wish to highlight a discussion point that was not followed up on from earlier in the chat, "I noticed Jenny made a good point about X earlier, what did everyone think about that?" This simple act, perhaps repeated at respectable intervals, is often enough to keep students on task.

Assigning roles

For students to consider themselves part of a community online, they must feel that they have a useful part to play. This is important not only for the individual, but it encourages the broadest response and the most diverse range of opinion. When you assign roles in a discussion, you support students in identifying a more explicit direction for their contributions.

Assigning roles is also a useful way of helping to embolden students to contribute online. Everyone has experienced putting on a mask as a child, feeling the power of taking on another identity. In a chat room it can achieve a similar result – taking on an explicit role helps encourage students to contribute and remain on task.

Assigning roles is also an effective way of encouraging rigour in student responses, particularly those that are reluctant or need additional stimulus. There are dozens of ways you might approach this, but I've suggested some below that I believe to be particularly effective. I've found Dr Edward de Bono's Six Thinking Hats work helpful in determining different types of roles for my students.

Remember that if you are using the Thinking Hats approach as intended and wish to explore an effective use of parallel-thinking methods, students should be encouraged to swap roles during the discussion. This ensures that you're making the "fullest use of everyone's intelligence and experience" (De Bono, 2022). It's also crucial that you explain this notion to students, to remind each of them that they have their own particular skills and a breadth of experience to draw on.

Devil's advocate
A role for a student that needs to explore a more complex argument.

Facilitator
What makes a good leader? You might suggest the student emulate a leader or facilitator they admire to help them get into the role.

Logical
Waits for all the facts to be presented, then uses logic and evidence to bring reason to the argument.

Community
This role broadens perspective. How does this issue manifest in the school community? In the local community? In the wider online community?

Emotional
This role allows the student to give a personal response to an issue.

Informational
A good role to assign early in discussion. A focus on facts, a gatherer of data. What do we have? What do we need?

Cautionary
In this role, the student must employ a careful approach to the subject, considering where harm may be caused. If, for example, the discussion is about starting a charity drive, the cautionary role encourages the student to focus on how the money is managed, safety concerns and issues of collective responsibility.

Imagine if
Students taking on this role need to look for the best things in the conversation and think laterally. Positive and encouraging, they should look for opportunities to broaden the discussion. Students working with this lens are charged with finding a different perspective, to inject some wonder and inquiry into the discussion. This is often best approached initially by simply encouraging use of the sentence stem 'imagine if...'!

Assigning roles to students allows them a layer of protection, to be bolder, more logical, more emotional about a subject. Taking on roles encourages them to step beyond their perceived peer expectations. Students will nominate for roles they think they are best suited to, but ensure all students take on a variety of roles.

Eventually, students will hopefully adopt roles as they see a need. "We're discussing the school fete, so I'd better take a cautionary role to make sure we're thinking about safety on the day."

Polling and checks for understanding

When hosting a live discussion using a tool like Webex or Zoom, polling tools are a key feature that you can use to influence the direction and pace of conversation in the classroom, to check for understanding and provide students with a layer of protection.

If, for example, you are discussing community attitudes towards pollution in the local creek, you may stop the discussion for a swift vote. "Let's find out what we think as a group, what question should we ask and what should the possible answers be?"

In this way, students are asked to pause and consider what the focus of the discussion is, and to ensure all views are represented in the possible polling responses.

Polling allows all voices to be heard – and heard regularly. And when the more reluctant students see that their attitudes and opinions are aligned with their peers, or that their minority view is considered and acknowledged, that can be a powerful encouragement to greater participation.

An online polling tool can also introduce pace to a classroom conversation, encouraging discussion strategically in a particular direction to ensure the time you have is spent to best effect. You can introduce numerous short sharp polls to direct the conversation towards the outcomes you're working towards.

Checking for understanding is critical and polling is an important tool in supporting collective understanding of where you're up to as a class, and where you need to go next. It's easy to assume student attitudes or the strength of understanding in an online space where attitudes are easily masked.

Think about how much you gain from physiological feedback in a classroom setting: student faces frowning or body language that suggests disengagement can be revealing. There are a myriad of small tells that reveal students are engaged, confused, anxious, frustrated or bored. Many of these simple indicators that become muscle memory for teachers are absent in the online space.

Polling tools give teachers a way to democratise that ongoing observational assessment and are a wonderful way for students to contribute with a layer of protection. Polling allows them to put forward a view to enable you to gauge quickly and simply whether the class is ready to shift up a gear or needs more time on a particular topic.

Used regularly, students become used to providing frequent feedback that's invaluable to your planning and to classroom cohesion. There's a simple but significant strength in being able to determine quickly and easily the temperature in the room. In a physical classroom you might use a method like 'fist to five' where students indicate with one hand their level of self-determined confidence or competence on a subject with one finger indicating low understanding. This still relies on students being willing to put up a hand and indicate they need help. In the online space, frequent and brisk anonymous polls enable you to determine that in a way that protects those students that need more support but that also builds a sense of the value of their contribution.

Polling tools are also a wonderful way for introducing ranking tasks effectively and efficiently. Simply choose a polling tool with multiple choice selections and allow students to rank information in order of importance or influence. For example, you may be trying to determine the importance of a sequence of events in a novel or you might wish to establish the correct sequence of actions in a science experiment.

Writing polling questions and answers doesn't have to be time-consuming. If you want to move a conversation along quickly with frequent polls, try simply setting your polling question to 'Make your choice' and your possible answers to 'A', 'B' and 'C'. All you need to do then is ask your question and remind students what each choice represents. Once the votes are in, discuss the results and then you can quickly clear the poll and use the same question and answers again and again. You'll find you can pose dozens of questions quickly and easily in sequence in this way.

Using polling tools in online discussions allows you to gauge a shift in opinion for any issue. You may, for example, wish to poll students in a 'what we know now' activity, on their opinions of a subject they are about to explore. For example, if you were exploring pollution, you may poll students to determine how many were aware of it in their local area.

Polling tools are a very effective way of revealing to students how readily they may shift opinion on an issue. When you conduct one before debating an issue, and then another after the facts have been presented and opinions discussed, you can determine the effectiveness of the argument in engendering a shift in perspective.

Key takeaways

- Consider how well you are using knowledge from digital interactions over the course of your learning sequence.
- Having strategies such as projecting and intruding can greatly enhance the interactions you can achieve in discussion spaces.
- Have key strategies for isolation and low participation ready, allowing you to respond effectively to a spectrum of interactions you can anticipate in shared spaces.

Sum it up

The complexity and scale of online interactions between students in synchronous and asynchronous spaces can be notable and varied. Have strategies in place in anticipation – and be prepared for a slow and considered transition for some students.

Put it into action

Employ one of the strategies from this chapter in your next three synchronous lessons.

Clarify how you will determine success in your use of that strategy.

Conclusion

This book, *Simple Tools*, offers a new way to think about teaching and learning with digital resources in the classroom. It attempts to define and distinguish impacts in the classroom stemming from poor digital tool design and selection, to clarify factors that influence our success and suggests a process through which to pursue change.

Selecting digital tools that have a clear purpose and do one thing well allows us to discern their appropriate alignment more easily with content and a pedagogical approach. By choosing simple tools that have IMPACT, we also help to reduce cognitive load and demand less of working memory.

By pairing this approach with classroom and visible thinking routines, I believe we have an accessible framework that facilitates improved clarity in the purpose and employment of digital tools for teachers and students.

The impacts of poor digital tool choice are profound. This method encourages reflection and agency, helping your students to think more strategically about how they use technology and guiding you to recognise the best digital tools for the task at hand.

How will you know whether you've succeeded? How will you know when your students have gained a tight grasp of the digital tools they use, and an increasing accomplishment in using them in combination to solve each problem they are confronted with?

The answer is surprisingly simple at first glance. The more you use a tool, the more familiar it becomes. The greater your proficiency, the more significant your conceptual understanding. In short, the more you get to know a thing and use it in a purposeful and reflective way, the more you understand its broader applications and its limitations.

Another natural outcome, of course, for students that wield these simple tools with greater intricacy, certainty and understanding, is that they will also reach for digital tools with increasing complexity.

This reflects your students' capacity to adapt. It's also a step forward that won't occur in a linear fashion. You'll find like many learning experiences, that this may occur haphazardly, with unanticipated leaps of attainment and regression.

The same simple purpose and understanding you place with a simple tool can also be applied with a tool that has a little more complexity – it's just that this additional path towards complexity comes with equally and additionally complex metacognitive steps. The challenge is to retain the lessons learnt from employing simple tools and apply them to more intricate digital resources.

Electing to use simple tools is not about taking shortcuts, dumbing down or reducing opportunities for more complex options. The Simple Tools approach is centred on finding digital resources that allow you to build awareness of their affordances and employing them in the most straightforward purposeful way towards the achievement of a learning outcome.

Working out which digital tools will best suit your classroom can be challenging, and incorporating new strategies into your practice takes time – but it's an investment that's well worth making. I am confident that by adopting some of the advice in this book, you'll feel better prepared to select and embed digital resources that have a purposeful fit within your existing practice.

Visit www.sequencedlearning.com for updates and free resources as they become available.

I'd also love to hear from you, about your stories of shifting your practice and what challenges you've overcome on that journey. So, please feel free to reach out using the contact page on my site.

Happy teaching and learning!

Martin

Acknowledgements

It is an astonishing thing to love the work that you do, and I feel that there is no greater endeavour and no career more satisfying than teaching. I would also not be the teacher I am, without the support of my colleagues at VSV.

I could not have written this book without the valued guidance of my publisher Alicia Cohen and editor Rica Dearman.

Grateful and sincere thanks to Glen Pearsall, Mike Phillips, David Harrison and Royan Lee for their honest appraisals of this work and their feedback and friendship. Thanks also to John Sweller, who was generous enough to provide feedback on my reflections on cognitive load. And, of course, to Penni Russon, Fred, Fig and Avery, without whom I would not have the life I am so grateful for.

References

Albion, P, & Ertmer, PA (2002). 'Beyond the Foundations: The Role of Vision and Belief in Teachers' Preparation for Integration of Technology.' *TechTrends*, 46 (5), 34–38. ISSN 8756-3894

Anderson, LW, & Krathwohl, D (eds) (2001). *A Taxonomy for Learning, Teaching and Assessing: A Revision of Bloom's Taxonomy of Educational Objectives.* Longman, New York

Anderson, M, & Perrin, A (2017). 'Barriers to adoption and attitudes towards technology.' [online] Pew Research Center: Internet, Science & Tech

Barbour, MK, & Adelstein, D (2013). 'High-school students' perceptions of effective online course design.' *The Morning Watch*, 41 (1–2), 56–65

Beghetto, R (2020). 'On creative thinking in education: Eight questions, eight answers.' *Future Edge*, New South Wales Department of Education, 1, 67

Blythe, T, & Associates (2009). *The Teaching for Understanding Guide.* San Francisco, Calif: Jossey-Bass Publishers

Boyd, D, & Marwick, A (2009). 'The Conundrum of Visibility: Youth Safety and the Internet.' *Journal of Children and Media,* 3 (4), 410-414

Brualdi Timmins, AC (1998). 'Classroom Questions.' *Practical Assessment, Research, and Evaluation,* 6 (6)

Buzan, T, & O'Brien, D (2018). *Mind Map Mastery: The Complete Guide to Learning and Using the Most Powerful Thinking Tool in the Universe.* Watkins Publishing

Cherney, MR, Fetherston, M, & Johnsen, LJ (2018). 'Online Course Student Collaboration Literature: A Review and Critique.' *Small Group Research* (49)

Churches, A (2007). 'Educational Origami, Bloom's and ICT Tools.'

Churches, A (2008). 'Bloom's Taxonomy Blooms Digitally.' Tech & Learning. Retrieved from www.techlearning.com/news/bloom39s-taxonomy-blooms-digitally

Darling-Hammond, L, Austin, K, Cheung, M, & Martin, D (2003). 'Thinking about Thinking: Metacognition.' In Darling-Hammond, L, Austin, K, Ourcutt, S, & Rosso, J (eds). 'The learning classroom: Theory into practice.' (156-177). *A telecourse for teacher education and professional development.* Stanford University School of Education

Davis, FD (1989). 'Perceived Usefulness, Perceived Ease of Use, and User Acceptance of Information Technology.' *MIS Quarterly,* 13 (3), 319-340

De Bono, E (2022). *Six Thinking Hats.* Kindle Edition

Dignath, C, & Büttner, G (2008). 'Components of fostering self-regulated learning among students. A meta-analysis on intervention studies at primary and secondary school level.' *Metacognition Learning,* 3, 231-264

Duffy, TM, & Cunningham, DJ (1996). 'Constructivism: Implications for the Design and Delivery of Instruction.' In Jonassen, DH (ed), *Handbook of Research for Educational Communications and Technology.* NY: Macmillan Library Reference USA

Elmore, R (2007). *The Age*, Letters to the editor, 27 August. Retrieved from bluyonder.wordpress.com/2007/09/24/teaching-isnt-rocket-science

Entwistle, NJ, & Peterson, ER (2004). 'Conceptions of learning and knowledge in higher education: Relationships with study behaviour and influences of learning environments.' *International Journal of Educational Research*, 41, 407–428. DOI:10.1016/j.ijer.2005.08.009

Ferdig, RE, Cavanaugh, C, Dipietro, M, Black, EW, & Dawson, K (2009). 'Virtual Schooling Standards and Best Practices for Teacher Education.' *Journal of Technology and Teacher Education*, 17 (4), 479–503. Waynesville, NC USA: Society for Information Technology & Teacher Education

Gregori, EB, Zhang, J, Galván-Fernández, C, & De Asís Fernández-Navarro, F (2018). 'Learner support in MOOCs: Identifying variables linked to completion.' *Computers & Education*, 122, 153–168

Harkins, S, & Petty, R (1982). 'Effects of Task Difficulty and Task Uniqueness on Social Loafing.' *Journal of Personality and Social Psychology*, 43, 1214–1229

Harris, J, & Hofer, M (2009). 'Instructional planning activity types as vehicles for curriculum-based TPACK development.' In Maddux, CD (ed) *Research highlights in technology and teacher education 2009* (99–108). Chesapeake, VA: Society for Information Technology in Teacher Education (SITE)

Hattie, JAC (2009). *Visible Learning: A Synthesis of Over 800 Meta-analyses Relating to Achievement*. New York, NY: Routledge

Ito, M, et al (2009). *Hanging Out, Messing Around, and Geeking Out: Kids Living and Learning with New Media*. Cambridge, Mass: MIT Press

Ito, M, Horst, HA, Bittanti, M, Herr-Stephenson, B, Lange, P, Pascoe, CJ, Robinson, L, Baumer, S, Cody, R, Mahendran, D, Martínez, K, & Perkel, D (2008). 'Living and Learning with New Media: Summary of Findings from the Digital Youth Project.' The John D and Catherine T MacArthur Foundation Reports on Digital Media and Learning

Johnson, DW, Johnson, T, & Stanne, MB (2000). 'Cooperative learning methods: A meta-analysis.' Minneapolis: University of Minnesota

Laurillard, D (2018). 'Teaching as a Design Science: Teachers Building, Testing, and Sharing Pedagogic Ideas.' In Voogt, J, Knezek, G, Christensen, R, Lai, KW (eds). *Second Handbook of Information Technology in Primary and Secondary Education.* Springer International Handbooks of Education, Springer, Cham

Lenhart, A (2009). 'Teens and Sexting.' Washington, DC: Pew Research Center's Internet & American Life Project

Lovell, O (2020). *Sweller's Cognitive Load Theory in Action.* John Catt Educational, Woodbridge

Mason, L, Boldrin, A, & Ariasi, N (2010). 'Epistemic metacognition in context: evaluating and learning online information.' *Metacognition Learning*, 5, 67–90

Mccrea, P (2015). *Lean Lesson Planning: A practical approach to doing less and achieving more in the classroom.* High Impact Teaching

Mccrea, P (2017). *Memorable Teaching: Leveraging memory to build deep and durable learning in the classroom.* High Impact Teaching

Mishra, P, & Koehler, MJ (2006). 'Technological Pedagogical Content Knowledge: A Framework for Teacher Knowledge.' *Teachers College Record*, 108 (6), 1017–1054

Mishra, P, & Koehler, MJ (2009). 'Too Cool for School? No Way! Using the TPACK Framework: You Can Have Your Hot Tools and Teach with Them, Too.' *Learning & Leading with Technology*, 36 (7), 14–18

Moreno, R, & Mayer, R (2007). 'Interactive Multimodal Learning Environments.' *Educational Psychology Review*, 19, 309–326

Muckerheide, P, Mogill, H, & Mogill, AT (1999). 'In search of a fair game.' *Mathematics and Computer Education*, 33 (2)

Nielsen, J (1994). 'Enhancing the explanatory power of usability heuristics.' Proceedings of the ACM CHI 1994 Conference. (Boston, MA, 24–28 April), 152–158

Nielsen, J (2020). '10 Usability Heuristics for User Interface Design.' Design Principles FTW

Nielsen, J, & Budiu, R (2012). *Mobile Usability*. Berkeley, CA: New Riders

Nielsen, J, & Molich, R (1990). 'Heuristic evaluation of user interfaces.' Proceedings of the ACM CHI 1990 Conference. (Seattle, WA, 1-5 April), 249-256

Olsen, R, & ideasLAB (2012). 'Understanding Pedagogies for Contemporary Teaching and Learning.' An ideasLAB White Paper

Pearsall, G (2018). *Fast and Effective Assessment – How to reduce your workload and improve student learning*. ASCD

Perkins, DN (2003). *Making Thinking Visible*, from www.pz.harvard.edu/resources/making-thinking-visible-article

Perkins, DN, Jay, E, & Tishman, S (1993). 'Beyond Abilities: A Dispositional Theory of Thinking.' *Merrill-Palmer Quarterly*, 39 (1), 1-21

Puentedura, RR (2006). 'Transformation, Technology, and Education in the state of Maine.' [Web log post, 18 August]

Puentedura, RR (2010). 'SAMR and TPCK: Intro to advanced practice.'

Puentedura, RR (2013). 'SAMR: Moving from enhancement to transformation.' [Web log post, 29 May]

Ritchhart, R, & Perkins, D (2008). 'Making Thinking Visible.' *Educational Leadership*, 65, 57-61

Ritchhart, R, Church, M, & Morrison, K (2011). *Making Thinking Visible*. Jossey-Bass Wiley. Project Zero's Visible Thinking: http://pz.harvard.edu/

Rogers, RR (2001). 'Reflection in Higher Education: A Concept Analysis.' *Innovative Higher Education*, 26 (1), 37-57

Runco, MA, & Kim, D (2018). 'The Four Ps of Creativity: Person, Product, Process, and Press.' DOI:10.1016/B978-0-12-809324-5.06193-9

Schraw, G (1998). 'Promoting general metacognitive awareness.' *Instructional Science*, 26, 113-125

Simonson, M, Schlosser, C, & Orellana, A (2011). 'Distance education research: A review of the literature.' *Journal of Computing in Higher Education*, 23 (2-3), 124-142

Sweller, J (2022). *Some Critical Thoughts about Critical and Creative Thinking.* The Centre for Independent Studies

Sweller, J, Ayres, P, & Kalyuga, S (2011). *Cognitive Load Theory.* Volume 1. New York: Springer

TeachThought (2017). '126 Bloom's Taxonomy Verbs for Digital Learning.' Retrieved from www.teachthought.com/critical-thinking/126-blooms-taxonomy-verbs-digital-learning

Tishman, S, Perkins, DN, & Jay, E (1993). 'Teaching Thinking Dispositions: From Transmission to Enculturation.' *Theory into Practice,* 3, 147–153

Venkatesh, V, & Davis, F (2000). 'A Theoretical Extension of the Technology Acceptance Model: Four Longitudinal Field Studies.' *Management Science,* Vol 456, No 2

Weinert, FE, & Schneider, W (eds) (1995). *Memory performance and competencies: Issues in growth and development.* Lawrence Erlbaum Associates, Inc

Weldon, P (2009). 'The AISV CyberCulture Survey.' (Research Brief No 3.01). Melbourne: Association of Independent Schools Victoria

Wikimedia Commons, retrieved from: commons.wikimedia.org/wiki/File:The_SAMR_Model.jpg

www.ingramcontent.com/pod-product-compliance
Lightning Source LLC
Chambersburg PA
CBHW071522080526
44588CB00011B/1530